Kilimanjaro

Kilimanjaro
John Reader

 UNIVERSE BOOKS . NEW YORK

Published in the United States of America in 1982
by Universe Books
381 Park Avenue South, New York, N. Y. 10016

Text and photographs © 1982 by John Reader

82 83 84 85 86/10 9 8 7 6 5 4 3 2 1

Book design by Donald Macpherson
Printed in Italy

Library of Congress Cataloging in Publication Data

Reader, John.
    Kilimanjaro.
    1. Kilimanjaro (Tanzania)   I. Title.
DT449.K4R43   1982   916.78'26   82-8665 ✓
    ISBN 0-87663-397-1   AACR2

For Mark

Contents

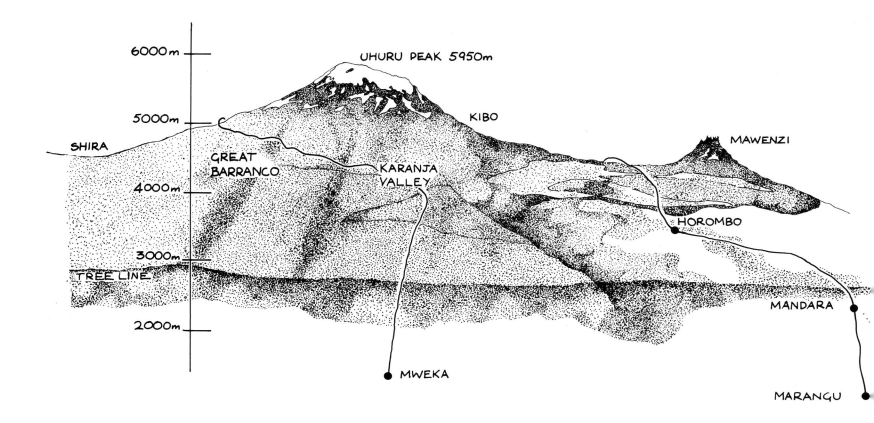

UHURU PEAK 5950m

6000m

5000m

SHIRA

KIBO

MAWENZI

GREAT
BARRANCO

KARANJA
VALLEY

4000m

HOROMBO

3000m

TREE LINE

MANDARA

2000m

MWEKA

MARANGU

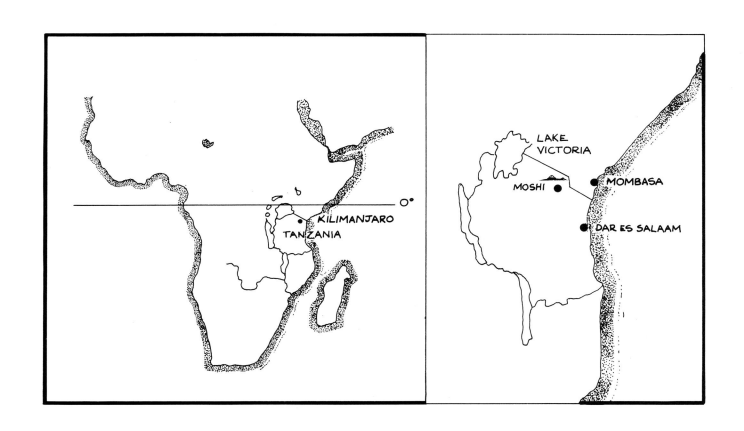

0°

KILIMANJARO

TANZANIA

LAKE
VICTORIA

MOSHI

MOMBASA

DAR ES SALAAM

Introduction

Dinner at the Marangu hotel is like a scene from one of those plays which gather an odd assortment of people in a remote hotel to await some unexpected, and probably unpleasant, event. Conversation is muted. The clock has stopped at twenty to nine; a faint sense of apprehension prevails. A small brass vase with a few flowers tastefully arranged stands on each table to be occupied that evening. There are several empty tables. The lights flicker because the mains electricity has failed again and the emergency generator is in operation. The young fellow sitting alone near the door takes a slim volume from his pocket whilst awaiting the second course. He is reading *Equus*.

The food as it arrives is wholesome and substantial. There are four courses, no menu, no choice. The waiters are silent and efficient, but cannot be hurried. Like the room, the furniture and the menu, they give a strong impression that time hardly touches this small corner of Tanzania. And indeed, the hotel has not changed much in the last fifty years. The establishment was a farm until 1932 and the present proprietor, Miss Erica von Lany, whose father came to Marangu from Europe in 1893, fondly remembers the time when the dining-room was the cowshed. Since then the farm has been satisfactorily adapted to its present function in most respects. The kitchen, however, remains as far from the dining-room as a farmer's wife would expect to be from the cows.

This evening, as on every evening since the hotel opened, most of the guests share the prospect of a unique experience. Tomorrow they will begin to climb Kilimanjaro, and it is this prospect that creates the sense of apprehension in the dining-room. The mountain is 5,860 metres high; at the summit the atmosphere contains less than half the oxygen available at sea level. Furthermore, the ascent entails a demanding five-day walk — eighty kilometres there and back. No one can be sure that he or she will reach the top; it is only certain that the attempt will be painful.

There are few — if any — of the world's natural wonders that offer quite the same opportunity for exploration and achievement as Kilimanjaro does. The experience of climbing the mountain is readily available to every tourist as a well-organized excursion. There are guides to lead the way, porters to carry the gear and stylish huts in which to spend the nights. Food can be provided, clothing and equipment can be hired. People of all shapes, sizes, ages, creeds and colour are attracted by the easy availability of the experience. They fly into Kilimanjaro International Airport with eager anticipation. They drive up to Marangu on the lower slopes with growing enthusiasm. Misgivings usually begin with the departure of the vehicles and the sobering realization that from now on achievement depends entirely upon physical effort of unprecedented severity. Few people who attempt to scale Kilimanjaro for the first time have ever exerted themselves quite so much before.

First misgivings might coincide with a first glimpse of the peak from the proximity of its slopes. So high, so beautiful — glistening above the tree-line. So enticing, but still so far away. Is this body fit enough to carry me there? Eighty kilometres and 5,800 metres add up to a long climb.

Because so many prospective climbers have little experience of either climbing or high altitude exertion, the Kilimanjaro National Park authorities have prepared a brief outline of some dangers that might be encountered. The printed sheet is posted in every hotel room and public place where prospective climbers might gather. It adds a biochemical dimension to doubts of physical capability. High altitude sickness produces headaches, weakness, nausea and vomiting. This is 'quite normal' and afflicts most climbers, the sheet advises. Less normal, but much more dangerous, is the pulmonary œdema which may follow excessive exertion at high altitudes. By reverse osmosis, liquid from the blood accumulates in the lungs, restricting the flow of oxygen in the other direction. First symptoms are not dissimilar to those of high altitude sickness, but the disability proceeds at an alarming rate and soon becomes unmistakable. A dry cough and blood-stained sputum are distinctive features of the disorder, the Park's information sheet vouchsafes; so are bubbling noises in the chest and a change in colour — lips, tongue, nose, ears and finger-nails turn blue. Without treatment death quickly ensues. Treatment, fortunately, requires only immediate removal to lower altitude and several days' rest.

Altitude, that obvious and unavoidable component of any worthwhile mountain excursion, is the most serious danger on Kilimanjaro, it seems. Gradual acclimatization is the best guarantee against its ill effects. One should not overdo things: 'If you climb fast and become exhausted the chances of achieving your aim are reduced and the dangers of high altitude sickness increased,' the sheet proclaims. Walk at a steady pace, stick to the recommended climbing schedule, drink four to six litres of water daily, do not weaken yourself by carrying for weaker members of the party; do not proceed above 2,750 metres with a sore throat, cold, cough or high temperature . . .

Thus the prospective climbers find themselves confronting an exhausting excursion with the advice that exhaustion is especially dangerous. The conundrum defies resolution, but it contributes to the sense of apprehension in the dining-room.

Not all the guests at dinner are prospective climbers. Some have just returned. Though not apart, they are separated by demeanour and bearing — they have been there. Three Germans at a table nearby, for instance, are easily distinguished. The young crewcut Bavarian among them consumes prodigious quantities of roast meat and vegetables. He reached the summit, but became giddy there, vomited and had to be led down by the guide holding his hand. His friends, husband and wife, gave up 900 metres from the top when the husband decided that the rushing of blood in his cheeks augured more hardship than he could bear. Overhearing all this two young Dutchmen resolved to resist every temptation even to attempt the ascent of the last 1,200 metres.

After dinner Miss von Lany gave a talk to the prospective climbers. In German, the majority language, she explained how they would walk from three to six hours each day on the way up and spend successive nights in Mandara, Horombo and Kibo Huts. They would begin the final ascent at 1.30 a.m., she told them, and return to Horombo Hut the same day; next day they would have lunch at Mandara and be back at the hotel by evening. Miss von Lany held a small, rather worn, sketch of the mountain painted on hardboard, on which she traced the route as she talked. The tone of her voice hinted at the boredom of repetition. Miss von Lany first climbed Kilimanjaro in 1926, when she was thirteen years old. She has spent her entire life in the shadow of the mountain, and fifty years ushering people up and down the peak. Thousands have spent evenings like this at the Marangu hotel, the sequence of events is always the same yet for every individual the experience is unique — unrepeatable. They are about to climb the highest mountain in Africa, something they have never attempted before, with no guarantee that they will succeed.

Climbing Kilimanjaro is an end in itself for most visitors, although some do have ancillary motives. Recently hang-gliders have taken to launching themselves from the peak — one was never seen again. In 1977 a young Spaniard actually rode a motorcycle to the top; several people have bicycled there and the summit was once the venue for the world's highest game of tiddlywinks. I wanted to photograph the mountain, especially the snows and the glaciers that line the crater. To do this effectively I would need to spend several days camped in the crater, which is two or three kilometres across and requires more time for proper exploration than a day visit allows. So mine was an independent trip. I would use parts of the tourist route, but I would also visit other places, sleeping in the open and walking right around the peak at between 3,500 and 4,000 metres, which ought to guarantee adequate acclimatization for the final climb to the summit and some nights camped in the crater.

In London it had all sounded simple enough. I assembled suitable clothing, rucksack, quantities of freeze-dried food and a number of slabs of mint cake (inseparably associated with mountains in my mind ever since I had read as a schoolboy of Hillary and Tensing nibbling a bar when they conquered Everest). At Marangu, however, I suffered some misgivings: I am not a mountaineer, I am not an athlete — just an average healthy city dweller. I once scrambled up to almost 5,000 metres on Mount Kenya, but I had never spent more than a couple of days at high altitudes, nor had I ever been entirely dependent upon my own physical resources for a long period. I would be accompanied by guide and porter, true, but apart from the climb my plans involved over 150 kilometres of walking — and *my* legs had to carry me, not theirs. So I brought some apprehension to the dining-room too.

Perhaps seeking a cliché to relate at this point, I looked for the snow-capped peak before going to bed that night. I suspect I had hoped to see it glistening magically in the moonlight, but I was spared. The peak was obscured by heavy cloud and rain seemed imminent. Considering its size,

Introduction

Kilimanjaro is remarkably difficult to see clearly. Cloud is the dominant factor these days, but mysterious obscurity has been the mountain's lot until comparatively recent times. In the earliest records the truth of its existence was confused by the inherent imprecision of geography at that time; later it was clouded first by myth and then by scientific prejudice. All in all it makes an interesting tale.

Discovery

The first view of Kilima-njaro from: The Kilima-njaro Expedition, H. H. Johnston 1886

In 45 AD an unknown author described the African coast in a work called the *Periplus of the Erythrean Sea*. He wrote: 'Beyond Opone (the modern Ras Hafun on the coast of Somalia). . . there are the small and great bluffs of Azania . . . twenty-three days' sail beyond there lies the very last market town of the continent of Azania, Rhapta . . . There are imported into these markets . . . hatchets and daggers and awls . . . there are exported . . . a great quantity of ivory and rhinoceros horn and tortoise shell.'

To the author of the *Periplus*, Rhapta was the end of the world, but a century later Ptolemy of Alexandria, astronomer and founder of scientific cartography, wrote of more lands to the south of Rhapta where 'man-eating barbarians' lived near a wide shallow bay. Ptolemy also wrote of a great snow mountain lying inland from Rhapta. No one is quite sure exactly where Rhapta was situated, but Ptolemy's 'great snow mountain' is surely Kilimanjaro.

After the Greeks came the Arabs, who were masters of East Africa from the sixth to the sixteenth century. The Arabs established many colonies along the coast, but they settled most permanently on the island of Zanzibar. The name means 'negro coast', and was first applied to the mid-African coast in general. The mainland eventually became known as the land of Zinj, however, whose King, a twelfth century Arab geographer records, resided at Mombasa.

The Chinese traded with the land of Zinj during Arab dominion. Fragments of pottery from the Ming dynasty have been found at several places along the coast and, more pertinent to our story, a Chinese chronicler of Chinese and Arab trade during the twelfth and thirteenth centuries remarked

1

that the country to the west of Zanzibar 'reaches to a great mountain'. In records spanning over one thousand years this is only the second remark that might refer to Kilimanjaro.

But, paucity of recorded comment notwithstanding, the mountain undoubtedly was seen by ever-increasing numbers of people as Arab influence spread into Central Africa. The Arabs themselves are not known to have ventured beyond the coastal belt, but their trade reached far inland and it sought not just ivory, gold and rhinoceros horn but another, more mobile, commodity as well — slaves.

Many of the sad caravans that brought untold thousands of Africans to the slave markets on the coast would have taken water from the permanent streams flowing from Kilimanjaro. The slopes of the mountain were inhabited by tribes who were themselves sometimes attacked by slave raiders or, in other cases, who acted as agents for the slave masters on the coast.

The Arab slave trade began before Christ and persisted for nearly 2,000 years. It swelled as the rise of Islam carried the Arabs to the forefront of history and brought them the riches of conquest. It became self-perpetuating as its wealth created more demand. The Arabs on Zanzibar and in the towns along the coast became exceedingly rich. They built fine lofty houses and surrounded themselves with the trappings of luxury. Their harbours were thronged with shipping, the warehouses were packed. They traded with the East and the Orient, but as yet they had no contact with Europe. Then, in 1497, Vasco da Gama followed the route his compatriot Bartholomew Diaz had taken around the Cape of Good Hope and proceeded along the coast to East Africa. He visited the Mozambique coast, Kilwa, Mombasa and Malindi and, though greeted with reserve, was impressed by the evidence of wealth that he saw.

On da Gama's return to Lisbon in 1499, the Portuguese rulers listened covetously to the accounts of such unexpected riches on the edge of a barbarous continent. By 1509 they possessed it all. The Portuguese conquest of East Africa was complete barely ten bloody years after they had discovered the country. And ten years later the Spanish geographer Fernandes de Encisco wrote: 'West of (Mombasa) is the Ethiopian Mount Olympus, which is very high, and further off are the Mountains of the Moon in which are the sources of the Nile. In all this country are much gold and wild animals . . .' The third reference to Kilimanjaro.

Portuguese occupation of the land of Zinj persisted for 200 years. If anything, it was even more oppressive than that of the Arabs. Where the Arabs had at least employed a measure of reciprocal trade in their exploitation of the Africans, the Portuguese primarily used force. Trade links were broken; the massacres of conquest were succeeded by demands for large annual tributes from regional rulers. Not surprisingly, the local inhabitants resisted and as the difficulties of maintaining such a distant colony were compounded by problems in Europe, Portugal's grip on the land of Zinj slackened. When they were finally expelled by Arab forces in 1699 they left behind unpleasant memories and very little of value.

The return of the Arabs to the land of Zinj coincided with the growth of the European slave trade. And not just trade in slaves to Europe but, much more significant, trade in slaves to places where European interests needed labour for their cotton and sugar plantations: America, the West Indies, Brazil, Mauritius and other Indian Ocean islands.

So the Arabs re-establishing themselves in Mombasa and Zanzibar found a lucrative trade awaiting their attention. They never again achieved the opulence they had enjoyed before the arrival of the Portuguese, but the mainland African population can hardly have noticed the difference: they were harassed and hunted throughout the continent. It is impossible to calculate how many slaves the Arabs shipped out of Africa. On the basis of reliable statistics for certain years it was once estimated that the trade across the Atlantic accounted for at least 12,000,000 people during the 150 years of the European trade. This of course included slaves from West as well as from East Africa. The Arabs traded almost exclusively to Arabia and across the Indian Ocean, but they were active for nearly 2,000 years. Their annual volume may never have matched that of the Atlantic trade, but the total effect of their constant and barbaric pillage could have been no less devastating.

Britain was the first nation to abolish the slave trade, which was made illegal by Act of Parliament in 1807 and in 1811 became an offence punishable by transportation to Australia. European and American abolition eventually followed (though not always with the alacrity it deserved) and the West African trade dwindled accordingly. But in East Africa it was another matter. The Arabs operating there were a law unto themselves, directed not by Europe or any other international influence but by the Koran, which actually condones slavery. Some subtle diplomacy would be needed to staunch the wound on the eastern side of Africa.

Britain established a diplomatic mission to Zanzibar in 1841, just as the leaders of the Industrial Revolution were beginning to perceive the need for fresh sources of raw materials. Of course the two developments did not coincide exactly, but each certainly furthered the other's end and together they provided stimulus and a potential source of information for a group of British academics who were sorely deprived of both commodities. The academics in question were the geographers trying to solve the riddles of Africa.

In the first half of the nineteenth century Africa was still very much a riddle. Maps of the day show northern and southern Africa, the west and east coasts in some detail but the rest — the vast interior of the continent — is blank, sometimes bearing the legend 'Unknown Parts'. And then there was the enigma of the Nile. Its source was unknown. Ptolemy and other classical geographers had said it flowed from some large lakes near the Mountains of the Moon in the centre of Africa, but there were no first hand reports of this and the ideas developed by geographers over the centuries to augment Ptolemy's statement were diverse to the point of absurdity. The maps with the legend 'Unknown Parts' were more honest.

In the absence of firm geographical evidence, argument ensued. Scholarly gentlemen scrutinized classical and Arab manuscripts for clues to the riddles of Africa and the Nile, but they inevitably produced different answers. The Mountains of the Moon were popular with all (though opinions differed as to where they were situated): one or two favoured the concept of large lakes from which the Nile flowed; others proposed a range of mountains closer to the east coast as the source.

Opinions were firmly held, arguments were conducted at length in the journals of the day. And then, because Arab slave traders were obliged to reach ever further inland for their merchandise, and because Britain was engaged in tedious diplomacy, a new source of information became available to British geographers — the reports of officials who had actually visited the coast and, through them, first-hand reports from caravan leaders who had travelled to the African interior. I say reports, in the plural, but precious few are recorded. One came from Khamis bin Uthman, who visited Britain in 1834 (supposedly at the behest of Seyyid Said who was then ruler in East Africa). Uthman met Palmerston and, among others, William Desborough Cooley, a most assiduous inquirer into questions of African geography. Cooley subsequently became a most prolific commentator on the subject and it is assumed that his pronouncements owed much to the conversations he had with Khamis bin Uthman.

Cooley favoured the idea that the Nile flowed from a large lake in Central Africa. In 1845 he published a lengthy article entitled *The Geography of N'yassi, or the Great Lake of Southern Africa investigated*. Apart from several bold statements on the geography of the region, Cooley's article also described the people living there. Among them were the people of Monomoezi, he wrote, who descended annually in large numbers to Zanzibar, trading copper, ivory and oil. The people of Monomoezi once used 'little balls like glass, of a reddish colour' for money, remarked Cooley. He continued: 'There is no difficulty in guessing what is here meant to be described. The most famous mountain of Eastern Africa is Kirimanjara, which we suppose, from a number of circumstances to be the highest ridge crossed on the road to Monomoezi. The top of this mountain is strewed all over with red carnelian, the rounded pebbles of which were doubtless the money referred to. The importation of beads has probably caused the disappearance of the carnelian currency,' Cooley concluded. Kirimanjara, strewn with carnelians, is surely Kilimanjaro, and Cooley's remark thus becomes the fourth known record of the mountain up to that time.

But while armchair geographers devised their grand schemes from second and third-hand reports, explorers adopted a more direct approach to the riddle of Africa. During the 1820s and '30s several attempts were made to reach the East African interior, though with little success. In 1824 a British naval officer, Lieutenant Reitz, succumbed to malaria before even passing beyond the estuary of the Pangani river he had been instructed to explore. In the 1830s Cooley himself persuaded the government, the Royal Geographical Society and some industrialists to fund an expedition. No doubt he expected to confirm his belief that the Nile flowed from his Lake N'yassi, but his prospectus placed rather more emphasis on the probability that new sources of iron, copper and timber would be discovered. Though adequately supported the expedition flopped. For reasons not entirely clear its leader, Captain Alexander (Cooley did not participate), abandoned the project in South Africa.

However, where military expertise, commercial interest and geographers' curiosity failed, Christian zeal eventually succeeded. Confronting sickness and danger with little more than their Bibles and umbrellas, Protestant missionaries were the first white men to venture beyond the comparative security of the East African coast. Their success was due entirely to the ambitions and extraordinary determination of Johann Ludwig Krapf, a Doctor of Divinity from Tübingen, working in Africa at the instigation of the London-based Church Missionary Society.

Krapf was connected with the CMS from 1837 until 1855. His first mission was to Abyssinia where, for a number of years, he endeavoured to bring the word of God to the Galla tribe. In 1843 internal politics forced the closure of the Abyssinia mission, whereupon Krapf suggested that, rather than abandon entirely his attempts to convert the Galla, he should travel down the East African coast in search of a base from which he might venture inland and approach the Galla from the south. The CMS concurred. Johann Krapf and his young wife, Rosine, arrived in Zanzibar on 7th January 1844. Krapf already spoke Arabic and soon became proficient in Swahili, the predominant language of the coastal people. His enquiries and brief excursions from Zanzibar revealed an almost unbounded potential for evangelical work — 'I can truly say that there are innumerable heathens who can be reached from this coast,' he wrote to the CMS. In March 1844 Krapf and his wife moved to Mombasa; thereafter his letters and journal become a harrowing tale of hardship and suffering.

Uhuru Peak, summit of Kilimanjaro, highest point in Africa, seen through clouds rising from the south-western slopes

Above and right: the southern glaciers

Below: the western glaciers, from the Shira Plateau

Opposite: the Great Barranco at 4,500m, south-west Kibo

Left: giant groundsels at 4,500m

Above: views of Kibo across the south-west shoulder

Previous page: Kilimanjaro summit, swathed with evening cloud above the Karanja Valley
Above: the summit at dusk from the Great Barranco wall at 4,000m

Rosine was pregnant when they left Zanzibar. She gave birth to a daughter on 6th July while both she and her husband were suffering from severe attacks of malaria. The baby was born well, but her mother's health quickly worsened. On the 9th she became convinced she was about to die, but her faith afforded no comfort. 'She wept bitterly,' her husband later wrote, 'she complained . . . of her heart being dry and cold without the slightest feeling of the Lord's sweet presence . . . "Oh my Saviour," she exclaimed, "I am not worthy of being in the midst of paradise, but let me only have a little place on its skirts . . .".' Krapf consoled and pacified her. He lay on a couch beside her bed, himself so prostrated by fever that when Rosine died some hours later it was only with the greatest effort that he could rise up to convince himself that she was really dead. His daughter died of fever five days later and was buried beside her mother on the mainland.

Krapf's missionary zeal provided a measure of solace for his loss. He wrote to the CMS committee chairman: 'Tell them, my dear Sir, that there is on the East African coast a lonely grave . . . This is a sign that you have commenced the struggle with this part of the world, and as the victories of the Church are stepping over the graves . . . of her members, you may be the more convinced, that the hour is at hand, when you are summoned to work upon the conversion of Africa from the East.'

In the same letter Krapf put forward an ambitious scheme for introducing the word of God to the heart of Africa. He believed the continent could be crossed in a walk of 900 hours and suggested: 'Let us place six missionaries at every hundred hours distance, and we shall be able to occupy the whole continent from east to west with the small number of fifty-four messengers of peace. Let us send out annually six of them and the whole space may be filled up in nine years . . . The way from Mombasa is open as far as to Djagga,' he wrote, drawing upon information gained locally. 'We can place two on the immediate coast, two others at Taita, a town situated on a high mount, three or four days' journey from here, and the rest at Djagga, where they will be able to make enquiries for the country beyond . . .'

In the six months following his wife's death Krapf translated the whole of the New Testament into Swahili, compiled a short grammar and dictionary of the language and made some exploratory journeys. But he made no converts to Christianity. Most of the town dwellers were committed to Islam. In the villages people first of all suspected Krapf of some ulterior motive and, when placated, manifested little interest in the word of God. Krapf ultimately concentrated his attention on the Wanika, a tribe living a little beyond Mombasa whose name means 'people of the bush' — a derogatory term in Swahili. Krapf was soon disillusioned with the Wanika. He was 'grieved in witnessing the drunkenness and sensuality, the dullness and indifference'; he noted that 'in general the Wanika are a lying, talking, drinking, superstitious, selfish and totally earthly minded people . . . they will sit together for a whole day engaged in useless talking, but when the missionary tells them about heavenly things, they either walk out of the room, or begin to talk of other matters . . .'

Beyond the Wanika lay the land of the Wakamba, a tribe whom Krapf found to be even 'greater drunkards than the Wanika . . . a most degraded people, swallowed up in the abyss of carnality.' Beyond the Wakamba roamed the elusive Galla.

Alone among heathens, his evangelical ambitions thwarted by indifference and difficulty, Krapf perhaps found comfort in contemplating the near impossible — his scheme for a string of missions across Africa. He never ceased trying to convert the people around him, but he was also determined to find the way to the heathens further inland. Information was scanty and occasionally conflicting.

Djagga seemed the most distant place to which access might be possible; some informants told him it lay north-west of Mombasa, others said south-west. Djagga apparently had been a central slave market for many years, where slaves from the interior were gathered and sold. Krapf learnt that the region was subject to excessive cold, which led him to speculate that possibly there were 'alpine heights in this part of East Africa'. On a map summarizing his knowledge, which he prepared in 1845, Krapf showed a mountain at Djagga, though he did not give it a name.

Meanwhile Krapf continued to suffer periodic attacks of malaria, some very severe. One bout lasted thirty-five days and when all available European medications were finished, Krapf resorted to a native prescription: a mixture of soot, red pepper, lemon juice and sap from a banana stem which was rubbed into incisions cut all over the body. 'It burns a little at first,' Krapf reported, 'but this is soon over, when the body must be washed in sea water.' Krapf believed the mixture had cured him and urged that medical authorities in Europe should investigate its properties. On other occasions malaria was compounded by boils breaking out all over the body. But Krapf found boils encouraging: 'This is rather a good sign,' he wrote, 'since my disease from within will be carried off externally.'

After two years of lonely suffering, Krapf's mission to Africa was supplemented by the arrival of Johann Rebmann, a Swiss who immediately impressed Krapf with his determination to bring Christian salvation to Africa. Rebmann contracted malaria very soon after arrival, and was confined to his bed for nearly a month. Meanwhile Krapf had arranged to move the mission to Rabbai Mpia, a Wanika village a short distance from Mombasa whose higher elevation promised more salubrious conditions. On 25th August 1845 Krapf and Rebmann left Mombasa for their new home. Neither man was entirely well. At first they took turns to ride their donkey, but before long Krapf was obliged to monopolize the beast. Rebmann tottered alongside for the remainder of the journey, very weak and scarcely able to climb the last slopes. 'Never was a mission begun in such weakness,' wrote Krapf, 'but so it was to be, that we might neither boast of our own strength, nor our successors forget that in working out His purposes, God sanctifies even our human infirmities to the fulfilment of His ends.'

With the arrival of Rebmann and the move to Rabbai Mpia, the Wanika were subjected to a resurgence of missionary fervour. They were invited, persuaded, cajoled to attend services each Sunday but saw little point unless food, drink or some gift was provided. Rebmann began school classes for the children, but the parents generally had some greater claim on their offspring's time. The tribal chiefs were urged to halt the practice of strangling infants born with deformities, and agreed, provided the missionaries would undertake to care for the unfortunate children. During their first year at Rabbai Mpia the missionaries offered Christian salvation to thousands, but none accepted (and this reluctance proved remarkably persistent — by 1859 the East Africa mission could claim just seven converts).

Surrounded by such discouraging evidence of their unfulfilled ambitions, Krapf and Rebmann turned with added enthusiasm to the still unblemished vision of a chain of missions across Africa. 'We must carry the message of salvation also to other quarters,' said Krapf, and one Saturday evening in September 1847 they decided to visit the Taita people living at Kasigau, a mountain 150 kilometres inland which could be seen from Rabbai on a clear day. Coastal traders regularly travelled to and from Kasigau but the Wanika chiefs were opposed to the missionaries going there. They said they would burn down the house of any tribesman who accompanied them and outlaw every accomplice. Negotiations to overcome such vehement opposition delayed the expedition for a week or two, but brought the missionaries into contact with Bwana Kheri, a well-respected caravan leader, who offered his assistance and, furthermore, said he was willing to take them to a place he called Jagga where, he added, 'the high mountain Kilimansharo . . . was visible.' This is the fifth mention of Kilimanjaro.

Rebmann and eight tribesmen finally set off for Kasigau on 16th October 1847; Krapf was too ill to accompany them. The journey marked the historic beginning of Europe's scramble into Central Africa, but it passed without incident. The party reached Kasigau in three days and Rebmann was immediately asked if he had come to build a castle. 'Yes,' he replied, 'but a spiritual one in which (the Taita) might be able to flee from the wrath of God.' He endeavoured to explain the elements of the Christian faith, using two sticks to describe the manner in which Christ had died. Rebmann had wanted to climb to the top of the mountain, where he hoped to obtain a view of the country to the west, but permission was withheld. He returned to Rabbai on 27th October, reporting that Kasigau would be a good place to establish a mission. The climate is excellent, with alpine air and water, he wrote, communications with the coast are good and the Taita 'are free from that savageness which would render it undesirable for one or two individuals only to reside in their country.'

Confident that the first link of the chain across Africa was now secure, the missionaries began to make plans for the second — Jagga — and encountered some strange information. The high mountain in Jagga called Kilimansharo was crowned with a white matter that resembled silver, Krapf was told in November 1847, and the mountain was full of djins and evil spirits. Gunpowder would not fire on its slopes; legs stiffened and people died from the bad effects of the djins. There was a legend of a King who once sent a large number of his subjects to examine the white matter. Only one returned. After his companions mysteriously perished during the ascent, this man — whose name was Sabaya — had continued upward until he reached a large door studded with iron spikes. The door stood open but Sabaya was too weak and frightened to enter. He retreated, hands and feet destroyed, crippled for life. The caravan leader Bwana Kheri claimed to have met the man.

The Governor of Mombasa Fort referred to these legends when Krapf sought official approval in April 1848 for an expedition to Jagga. Krapf writes: 'The Governor had some scruples with regard to ascending the Mount Kilimandsharo in Jagga. He said the mount was full of djins. I replied that Mr Rebmann did not go to Jagga on account of seeing the mountain, or of searching for the silver which was said to be on the top of the mount. As to the djins, it was ridiculous to frighten a European by such stories. If people did suddenly die on that mount, it must be ascribed to other causes than the haunting of djins. There was probably some fine sand, which giving way would suddenly gulp down a heedless traveller, or the rarified air might endanger him at a great height of the mountain — which the Swahili not understanding attributed to the operation of the djins.' The Governor smiled at this interpretation, Krapf reports, and gave consent for the journey.

The missionary's expedition left for Jagga on 27th April 1848. Rebmann was accompanied by Bwana Kheri and eight tribesmen. Once again Krapf was too ill to travel, and separation distressed him: 'Mr Rebmann is . . . starting on his perilous and interesting journey to Dshagga, several hundred miles from here,' he wrote. 'It will cost us a good deal of money (140 or 160 dollars), but the journey will be full of interest, if the Almighty brings the dear brother back in safety . . . These parting moments are connected with peculiar feelings . . . which our friends at home can hardly understand. Here we are in the midst of African heathenism, among wilful liars and trickish men, who desire only our property whilst we wish to . . . convey the message of a Saviour. The only earthly friend whom I have, and whom he has, does at once disappear, each of us setting his face towards . . . our respective destinations while our friends at home do not know where we are, whither we go, and what we are doing.'

Rebmann quickly proceeded beyond Kasigau. The party lost their way in thorn thickets, slept where tribal wars had been fought years before, heard the growling of lions and were detained for some days in the company of Maina, a regional chief of the Taita. The people Rebmann encountered were surprised that he carried only an umbrella where before caravans were obliged to retain the protection of 500 armed men. In reply Rebmann observed that the Almighty had cleared the way for the diffusion of the Gospel . . . They left Maina's village with a gift of meat that attracted the hyenas; on 10th May they saw zebra, giraffe and rhinoceros, they passed pits dug to trap elephants and walked through sharp and spiky grass that cut Rebmann's feet. They camped that night to the south-east of Ngalia about 150 kilometres from the coast.

Next morning, 11th May, Rebmann notes: 'The mountains of Jagga gradually rose more distinctly to my sight. At about 10 o'clock (I had no watch with me) I observed something remarkably white on the top of a high mountain and first supposed it was a very white cloud in which supposition my guide also confirmed me, but having gone a few paces more I could no more rest satisfied with that explanation and while I was asking my guide a second time whether that white thing was indeed a cloud and scarcely listening to his answer that *yonder* was a cloud but what that white was he did not know but supposed it was *coldness* — the most delightful recognition took place in my mind of an old well-known European guest called *Snow*. All the strange stories we had so often heard about the gold and silver mountain Kilimansharo in Jagga, supposed to be inaccessible on account of evil spirits which had killed a great many of those who had attempted to ascend it, were now at once rendered intelligible to me, as of course the extreme cold, to which the poor natives are perfect strangers, would soon chill and kill the half-naked visitors. I endeavoured to explain to my people the nature of that "white thing" for which no name exists even in the language of Jagga itself, but they at first appeared as if they were not to trust my word. Soon after we sat down to rest a little when I read the 111th psalm at which I had just arrived in my daily reading. It made a singular impression on my mind in the view of the beautiful snow mountain so near the equator, and gave — especially the 6th verse — the best expressions to the feelings and anticipations I was moved with.' The verse reads: 'He hath shewed his people the power of his works, that he may give them the heritage of the heathen.'

Rebmann went on to Jagga, where he stayed several days at a village on the lower slopes of Kilimanjaro, but constant rain withheld a further glimpse of the snow-capped peak. He confirmed that prospects of establishing a mission in Jagga were good, and returned safely to Rabbai Mpia on 11th June 1848. His account of a snow-capped mountain near the equator was published in the *Church Missionary Intelligencer* of April 1849, and immediately brought new impetus to the controversy concerning the geography of inner Africa and the source of the Nile.

In the *Atheneum* magazine, the geographer Charles Beke offered Rebmann's report as proof that the Nile rose south of the equator on the east of the continent. 'The Nile has its origin in Mount Kilimanjaro,' he asserted. In a Presidential address to the Royal Geographical Society, W.J. Hamilton allowed that the discovery of a lofty mountain covered with perpetual snow so near the equator was indeed remarkable and gave 'additional strength to the arguments of those who look for the sources of the Nile to the south of the equator.' But William Desborough Cooley, author of exhaustive treatises on the geography of inner Africa, confidant of Khamis bin Uthman and firm believer that the Nile flowed from a Central African lake, did not agree. Nor did he agree that Kilimanjaro stood where Rebmann had said it did, nor that the mountain was capped with snow, nor even that the substance on top was white in colour.

Cooley gave his objections in the *Atheneum* a week after Beke's remarks had appeared. His main target was Beke's contention concerning the source of the Nile, but he spared the missionary no scorn, ascribing his sighting of Kilimanjaro to a fortuitous combination of imagination and poor eyesight: 'In Mr Rebmann's account of the "eternal snows" . . . we miss the proportions of nature and the colour of reality,' wrote Cooley. Such a mountain would be a stupendous mass, he observed, 'but Mr Rebmann's sketch is unaccountably feeble and obscure . . . He first describes it at a distance of some twenty-five miles; he sees something white, and concludes it to be snow . . . The white something soon grows to be "a beautiful snow mountain"; the snow becomes "eternal snow" and "everlasting winter".' These remarks, wrote Cooley, 'are merely amplifications of a favourite idea, not resting at all on the evidence of the senses . . . I deny altogether the existence of snow on Mount Kilimanjaro. It rests entirely on the testimony of Mr Rebmann, . . . and he ascertained it, not with his eyes, but by inference and in the visions of his imagination.'

Cooley re-amplified his own favourite idea of Kilimanjaro in the same article: 'That mountain is famed for its great height and for the red carnelian strewed over it . . . Nay further, the name of the mountain is given not only to its characteristic mineral but to similar objects, and, hence, along the coast, red coral is very commonly, if not generally, called Kirimanjara.' 'The mountain in question is well known to the Swahili traders,' wrote Cooley, 'and it is called, not the White Mountain, or the Snowy Mountain, but Kirimanjara, a name associated in popular language with a red production.'

Despite his bizarre reasoning and aggressive manner, Cooley's objection to the missionary's wholly accurate eye-witness account of the snow-capped Mount Kilimanjaro standing three or four degrees south of the equator gained more authoritative support than it deserved. Twelve years passed before further evidence required various eminent gentlemen to concede the accuracy of Rebmann's report — though Cooley never did.

Exploration

Kilima-njaro, showing both its snow-capped peaks from: The Kilima-njaro Expedition, H. H. Johnston 1886

Johann Rebmann was about forty kilometres from Kilimanjaro when he first saw the snowy peak in May 1848. By the time the account of his discovery was published in the *Church Missionary Intelligencer* a year later, he had already returned twice to the Chagga region, to use the modern spelling, and had enjoyed many fine views of Kilimanjaro. In December 1848 he passed so close under the mountain that he found the nights as cold as Germany in November and could see the 'majestic snow-clad summit' even by night, in the light of the moon. On that journey Rebmann noted that the mountain comprised two principal summits with a space between them forming 'as it were, a saddle . . . three or four leagues from east to west. The eastern summit is lower, and pointed,' Rebmann reported, 'whilst the western and higher one presents a fine crown, which, even in the hot seasons, . . . remains covered by a mass of snow.'

Rebmann learned that while the coastal people understood the name Kilimanjaro to mean 'mountain of greatness', it could also be translated as 'mountain of caravans' (*kilima* — mountain, *jaro* — caravans), a landmark for caravans that could be seen from afar everywhere. The Chagga people, however, called the peak Kibo, which Rebmann understood to mean 'snow' in their language (contrary to his earlier understanding that the Chagga had no such term).

Rebmann made a third journey to Chagga in April 1849, resolved to travel far beyond, to Uniamesi — the next stage in the projected chain of missionary stations across Africa. King Mamkinga at Machame on the slopes of Kilimanjaro had promised to assist this ambitious expedition to the interior. In anticipation of a long and expensive journey, the party that left Rabbai Mpia with Rebmann was thirty strong, and carried large quantities of cloth and beads and other goods to be dispensed as gifts, and in return for services. But the expedition was not a success. The rainy season had just begun and, as Rebmann recounts, his solitary umbrella was not enough to protect the party from the downpours that engulfed it each night. Rivers were flooded, rhinoceroses were troublesome and when Rebmann reached Machame he found King Mamkinga far less helpful than had been anticipated. In fact, by procrastinating, and by demanding ever more gifts for himself in advance of the assistance he promised, the King reduced Rebmann's stock to the point where he had not the means to proceed further even if Mamkinga's assistance was forthcoming. Rebmann wept; the King promised ivory in return for the goods he had appropriated but, when it was asked for, replied that a man of God ought not to wish for such things. Afflicted by despair, fever, dysentery and the constant rain, Rebmann abandoned hope of proceeding to Uniamesi and returned to Rabbai. On leaving Machame the party was afforded the custom of being spat upon by their hosts to the accompaniment of the words 'Go in peace', but they were required to pay for this courtesy with their few remaining beads.

The snows that crown Kilimanjaro are not mentioned in Rebmann's account of his unhappy attempt to reach Uniamesi via Chagga. Very probably they were obscured by cloud throughout his visit, and certainly there were other things to engage his attention. The missionaries never returned to Chagga, though they explored other routes to the interior. In July 1848 Krapf, his health restored, had reached Fuga in the Usambara mountains to the south of Mombasa. In November 1849 he set out for the land of the Wakamba, in the north-west. On 10th November he saw Kilimanjaro, a distant view, but he could clearly see that the white crown must be snow. 'All the arguments which Mr Cooley has adduced against the existence of such a snow mountain, and against the accuracy of Rebmann's report, dwindle into nothing when one has the evidence of one's own eyes before one; so that they are scarcely worth refuting,' Krapf wrote at a later date. Krapf saw Kilimanjaro several times; and on 3rd December 1849 he saw Mount Kenya, the second snow-capped mountain of East Africa.

Accounts of the discovery of Mount Kenya and of the confirmatory sightings of Kilimanjaro were duly published in the *Church Missionary Intelligencer*. Though couched in florid if not evangelical terms, and though lacking the figures and facts deemed essential to reliable geographical observation, there was no good reason to suppose that the missionaries' reports were anything less than the genuine accounts of men who had seen the snow-capped mountains with their own eyes. Both men were familiar with the sight of snow on the Alps, so they were hardly likely to mistake the phenomenon when encountered elsewhere. Krapf had seen Kilimanjaro and Kenya from a distance; Rebmann, furthermore, had traversed the lower southern slopes of Kilimanjaro and had seen the snowy peak repeatedly over a period of days from a distance of less than thirty kilometres.

Even so, the missionaries' eye-witness accounts did not convince the experts 5,000 kilometres away in England that snow-capped mountains existed in eastern equatorial Africa. Foremost among those denying the contention was William Desborough Cooley. Cooley never again suggested that the summit of Kilimanjaro was strewn with red carnelian, but he clung tenaciously to his belief that the mountain was not high enough to be covered in perpetual snow. His argument was based firstly on his interpretation of classical and Arab reports of the region (and it is curious that he should have accepted these second, third and — who knows? — perhaps even fourth and fifth-hand accounts against the validity of eye-witness accounts from contemporaries); and secondly on the inconsistencies and misinterpretations he drew so assiduously from the missionaries' reports. If

Rebmann said the mountain was 20,000 feet (6,000 metres) high and Krapf said 12,500 feet (3,800 metres) then both must be wrong and the mountain was not covered in snow. This was the gist of Cooley's argument, presented most fully in a book entitled *Inner Africa Laid Open* which he published in 1852. Geographers subsequently came to call the book 'Inner Africa Shut Fast', but for a time its arguments found favour in certain quarters. Sir Roderick Murchison, President of the Royal Geographical Society during its heyday of African exploration, was 'to a great degree incredulous' of the proposition that there could be 'lofty snow-covered mountains under the equator'. Sir Roderick confessed himself persuaded by Cooley that the missionaries 'might have been misled'.

And Richard Burton, though no friend of Cooley's, found the missionaries less than convincing. In Cairo, while they were en route to and from Europe respectively, Burton had listened to Krapf speaking of the source of the Nile, the Mountains of the Moon, and of Kilimanjaro. 'These stories,' he wrote to the Secretary of the RGS in November 1853, 'reminded one of a de Lunatico.'

The missionaries must have found these doubts absurd. Certainly they could rest secure in the evidence of their own eyes, but their case slipped a peg or two in 1856 when they published a map of East Africa showing not just the features they had seen, but also some they had only heard about. This celebrated document was soon dubbed 'the slug map' by virtue of the great body of water it showed sprawling through twelve degrees latitude where we now know there are several separate lakes. The missionaries had produced their map on the basis of travellers' tales. While it might have won a measure of support from Cooley, who believed the Nile flowed from a single large inner African lake, it surely alienated those who believed in the existence of several lakes, and cast a shadow of doubt over the snow-capped mountains.

The doubt deepened in December that year when David Livingstone, just returned from his epic solitary journey across Africa, told the Royal Geographical Society of some white mountains he had encountered in the Zambezi valley. 'From the description I got of its glistening whiteness, I imagined that it was *snow*,' Livingstone told his audience, 'but when I observed the height of the hill, I saw that snow could not lie on it . . . The white mountains . . . are masses of white rock somewhat like quartz,' he said.

In an address to the same meeting Sir Roderick Murchison enlarged upon these remarks: 'It seems that the range of white-capped hills which Dr Livingstone examined, trended towards those so-called Mountains (of the Moon),' he said, 'and it may prove that the missionaries, who believe that they saw snowy mountains under the equator, have been deceived by the glittering aspect of the rocks under a tropical sun.'

Meanwhile the Royal Geographical Society had determined to resolve the vexing uncertainties of Central African geography by sponsoring an expedition to the interior. Richard Burton was assigned to lead the expedition, John Hanning Speke was invited to join it. Both men were army officers, resourceful and reliable. In 1854 Speke had participated in Burton's exploration of Somalia. A total of one thousand pounds was placed at Burton's disposal for the East Africa expedition. He was instructed to make his way to the lake that reputedly lay inland, determine its extent and character, explore the surrounding country and record all details of geography, towns, tribes, minerals, products and commerce, leaving nothing to memory alone. Burton and Speke arrived in Zanzibar — first staging-post of their expedition — on 19th December 1856.

In May 1857 Sir Roderick Murchison delivered his Presidential Address to the Royal

Geographical Society, in the course of which he said: 'Let us hope that the journeys now in progress by our clever and adventurous traveller Captain Burton (shall inform us) whether the large lake Uniamesi be not the real feeder of the Nile, or if there really be lofty snow covered mountains under the equator, as descried in the distance by our missionaries.'

In arranging the expedition the Royal Geographical Society had sought the advice of the Church Missionary Society and, indeed, had agreed that Johann Rebmann should accompany and assist Burton on his exploration of the interior. Burton was instructed to contact the missionary immediately on arrival, 'to mutually concert' operations for the expedition, and 'to give great weight to the counsel of Mr Rebmann.' Burton was also advised that Rebmann would be 'pursuing his avocation as a missionary' while on the expedition.

But it was not fated that the reverend gentleman should accompany the expedition. By 1857 the activities of marauding Masai tribesmen had made travel through the Mombasa hinterland a most dangerous undertaking, it seemed, and Mr Rebmann was not sure that he wished to accompany Burton. Moreover, 'the unhappy political interferences of Dr Krapf' (by which Burton meant Krapf's undercover attempts to hasten the end of the lingering Zanzibar slave trade) had incensed Arabs throughout the region. The British Agent in Zanzibar urged Burton not to associate with any missionary enterprise. In fact he told him that official and local co-operation would depend upon its exclusion from the expedition. Burton concurred, though he parted from Rebmann 'with regret', he wrote, for the missionary had not hesitated 'to throw open his ample stores of knowledge.'

With the route from Mombasa to the interior via Kilimanjaro closed by the Masai, and access from the coast opposite Zanzibar exceedingly difficult until the monsoon rains ceased in June, Burton and Speke meanwhile familiarized themselves with 'the accidents of travel in this exceptional land'. In February they sailed down the coast to Pangani and walked from there to Fuga in the Usambara mountains, which Krapf had visited nearly nine years before. Both men returned with fever severe enough to require six weeks' convalescence. In Tanga they heard wild tales concerning the 'Aethiopic Olympus, Kilimanjaro', Burton reported. They were told that a city of brass had once been built there, and the mountain top encrusted with a dome of silver that shone with various and surpassing colours. But now, apparently, the mountain was inhabited by fiery beings who baffled man's adventurous foot: the mountain receded as the traveller advanced, the summit rose as he ascended; blood burst from the nostrils, fingers bent backwards . . . even the most adventurous were forced back.

All Burton's informants mentioned the intense cold of Chagga and Kilimanjaro, though those who spoke from hearsay alone usually wove the information into some colourful tale of the mountain. On the other hand, Burton found that travellers who actually had visited the region 'described the much vexed Aethiopic Olympus soberly and,' he concluded, 'correctly.'

Unfortunately Burton does not give an account of those sober and correct descriptions of Kilimanjaro. A surprising omission when set against the exhaustive, eloquent and unequivocal accounts he gave of so many other phenomena encountered on his travels. So we do not know whether the travellers reported a snow-capped peak to Burton, nor do we know whether Burton accepted the missionaries' account of one. Nowhere does he express his opinion at the time — though he left no doubt that the question was still open in his mind. When explaining that the Masai and the weather prevented his expedition proceeding directly to the interior via Kilimanjaro, Burton remarked that in the dry season, with an escort of a hundred musketeers and at the expense of £600 the traveller 'may, if sound in wind, limb, and digestion, reach the snowy region — if such exist — . . .'

Burton chose a more southerly route to the interior, where he was ill frequently and Speke discovered Lake Victoria, the ultimate source of the Nile.

Though Burton and Speke contributed little to the debate concerning the alleged lofty snow-covered mountain under the equator, the absence of definitive comment from such reputable sources in itself served to deepen and prolong the controversy. When their reports were read before the RGS in May 1859, Sir Roderick Murchison suggested that because the explorers had climbed no higher than 3,500 feet (about a thousand metres) on their journey to Usambara, they had 'cast slight further doubt' on the observations of Rebmann and Krapf. Murchison reminded the meeting of his preference for Cooley's version of East African geography. Another speaker, the distinguished geographer James MacQueen, spoke in support of the missionaries' view, but his argument is but briefly mentioned in the Society's Proceedings — not reported in substance as fairness might have demanded.

And so, ten years after the news was first published, the existence of permanent snow in eastern equatorial Africa was still denied.

While Burton and Speke attended to the mysteries of Central Africa at the behest of the Royal Geographical Society, in 1858 the British Government despatched another expedition to investigate African mysteries further south. It was led by Dr David Livingstone, then at the height of his fame. Livingstone intended to reach the interior by way of the Zambezi river which, he believed, would provide 'an open road for commerce and Christianity'. Six specialists accompanied Livingstone, including a young geologist, Richard Thornton, who was assigned to provide an authoritative assessment of the region's mineral potential, particularly in respect of coal.

The expedition was provided with £5,000 and a steam launch, but the launch was rather frail, and turbulent rapids made the Zambezi and its tributaries rather less easily navigable than Livingstone had hoped. He discovered Lake Nyasa (though forced to walk part of the way), but the Zambezi Expedition is more often noted for disharmony among its participants than for discoveries. Thornton did not take part in much of it. He remained at Tete, alone and ill with prickly heat and malaria, while the expedition's two doctors both accompanied Livingstone. Thornton was not yet twenty-one and had never been to Africa before, but Livingstone had little sympathy for either his innocence or inexperience; he found the young man 'incorrigibly lazy' and in want of 'good sense'. In June 1859 Livingstone dismissed Thornton and fined him six weeks' pay for inadequate work. Livingstone returned to the wilderness and Thornton, left to his own devices, displayed little of the inadequacy Livingstone had deplored. For twenty months he explored the Zambezi region on his own account. In March 1861 he sailed to Zanzibar where he met Baron Carl Claus von der Decken, a twenty-seven-year-old Hanoverian aristocrat of considerable means and a determined ambition to explore the African interior.

Geographic and commercial curiosity concerning the African interior was not confined to Britain during the 1850s. The Germans were curious too. Their countrymen had led the way (though sponsored by a British missionary society); secular interests followed some years later, when the exiled King Ludwig of Bavaria commissioned Albrecht Roscher to investigate the mysterious 'inland sea'. Roscher arrived at Zanzibar in the autumn of 1858; he was twenty-two years old and his principal qualification for African exploration seems to have been the university thesis he had prepared on Ptolemy and the trade routes of Central Africa.

The excitement of science and exploration also had caught the attention of Baron von der Decken. After a spell of hunting in Algeria the Baron had abandoned a military career in favour of his new interests. In 1860 he sailed for Zanzibar, where he expected to join Roscher in return for financing further exploration. On arrival, however, he learned that Roscher had been murdered by tribesmen somewhere near the eastern shore of Lake Nyasa. Von der Decken immediately set off 'to rescue Roscher's effects and avenge his death.' He travelled 250 kilometres inland but achieved neither of his aims. Porters deserted and stole his possessions, villagers refused to sell him food, his armed escort was mutinous. The Baron returned to Zanzibar early in 1861, convinced that the Arab and tribal rulers had connived against him but nonetheless determined to explore the African interior. With the Nyasa route so firmly closed he sought an alternative target, and ultimately decided to visit Kilimanjaro where he would settle 'once and for all, the still disputed question of snow in tropical Africa'. It was, of course, around this time that Richard Thornton arrived in Zanzibar.

Thornton joined von der Decken's expedition. With a caravan of over fifty porters and servants (including the Baron's Italian man-servant and Thornton's personal slave) the two men left Mombasa for Kilimanjaro on 29th June 1861. They took the direct route and on 10th July encountered an example of the tribal behaviour that had persuaded Burton to take a more southerly route. Taita leaders challenged von der Decken for the expedition's trespass and the return of botanical specimens its members had collected. The Baron refused to pay compensation, at which 200 warriors threatened the party — 'roaring, howling, yelling, leaping' — as Thornton records. The Baron stood firm (but ordered his men to load their weapons). Eventually the caravan leader paid compensation from his personal stock, a move which placated the Taita and preserved the Baron's dignity.

Four days later, 14th July 1861, the explorers saw Kilimanjaro. The mountain 'shone out beautifully for a few minutes showing streaks of snow running down its sides at the bottom of numerous ravines to nearly the base of the upper cone,' Thornton wrote in his diary.

The Baron had hoped to lead his expedition triumphantly to the top of Kilimanjaro (indeed, his baggage had contained a celebratory bottle of champagne, though this had already been consumed one thirsty day en route to the mountain), but his ambition was first opposed by the local chiefs, and then thwarted by the reluctance of his porters to proceed above the rain forest. Nonetheless, von der Decken and Thornton spent nineteen days on and around Kilimanjaro. They did not succeed in climbing higher than 2,500 metres, but Thornton was able to record numerous observations of the snow-covered mountain. His sightings and subsequent calculations gave the main peak — Kibo — a height of between 19,812 and 20,655 feet (the correct figure is now known to be 19,340 feet or 5,860 metres), of which roughly the last 3,000 feet (900 metres) were permanently covered with snow. Mawenzi, the peak to the east of Kibo, was between 17,257 and 17,453 feet high according to Thornton (correct figure 17,562 feet or 5,321 metres). Geologically, the mountain was a mass of volcanic lava which had consolidated in the open air, Thornton deduced. The Shira Plateau and its crumpled peaks to the west of Kibo were the oldest part of the massif, he said, while Kibo was the youngest, with the north-east rim of its crater still intact and distinguishable.

These, and many more details of geology, geography, anthropology, botany, etc are recorded in Thornton's voluminous diaries of the Kilimanjaro expedition. These documents provided authoritative confirmation that a snow-capped mountain existed under the equator — thirteen years after Johann Rebmann had first observed the phenomenon. In November 1861 von der Decken wrote to Germany: 'Kilimanjaro is 21,000 (sic) feet high, and covered with permanent snow . . .'

Not long after returning from Kilimanjaro, Thornton was invited to rejoin Livingstone's expedition (though on less auspicious terms than before). He sailed from Zanzibar in March 1862, and died on the Zambezi of fever in April 1863, four days before his twenty-fifth birthday.

Von der Decken, meanwhile, had invited Dr Otto Kersten, a young German scientist, to assist him in the further exploration of East Africa. The Baron planned an ambitious expedition. He would return to Kilimanjaro, scale the peak, proceed thereafter to Lake Victoria, and return to Mombasa via Mount Kenya. In the event, tales of unfriendly Masai ranged along the route to Lake Victoria persuaded the Baron to confine his ambitions to Kilimanjaro, where the expedition arrived in November 1862. The Baron once again failed to conquer the peak, but did reach an altitude of 4,200 metres, where he experienced a fall of snow.

'So opportune a fall of snow,' protested William Desborough Cooley when von der Decken reported on his expeditions to Kilimanjaro. From his rooms in Bloomsbury Cooley peremptorily dismissed the Baron's reports. ' "The Sporting Baron" did not experience a fall of snow,' he told readers of the *Atheneum.* Nor had von der Decken 'communicated to the learned world a single particle of precise information of any kind.' In Cooley's view the Baron was an 'eccentric traveller' who had set out to confirm 'the vacillating, inconsistent accounts of the missionaries,' his countrymen, and had done so by odd and inexact scientific procedures.

But, though still afforded the privilege of publication, Cooley's obstinate views had lost all support. In print the Baron and his reports were defended as vigorously as Cooley attacked them. At the Royal Geographical Society, Sir Roderick Murchison conceded that Rebmann and Krapf had been right all along. In 1863 Baron Carl Claus von der Decken was awarded the Gold Medal of the RGS for his contributions to the geographical knowledge of inner Africa. In October 1865 he was murdered at Barbera while attempting to reach Mount Kenya by way of the Juba river; he was thirty-three years old.

Exploitation

Slavers revenging their losses from: The Last Journals of David Livingstone 1874

In the 1850s and early '60s, while the travels of Rebmann and Krapf attracted the attention of geographers and explorers, the evangelical endeavours of the missionaries inspired some other churches to despatch a few more messengers of God to lighten the dark soul of Africa. To Krapf's anger and dismay, the first to arrive (in early 1861) was a party of Jesuits: Catholics, whose worldly and colourful dogma, Krapf opined, would inevitably entice prospective converts from his strict Protestant creed and lead them straight to the devil.

The second party, sent by the United Methodist Free Churches of England a little later in 1861, was more to Krapf's liking. Indeed, he had encouraged their venture and actively assisted with the establishment of their mission in a tent sixteen miles from Mombasa. Of the four Methodist missionaries, three found conditions in Africa more difficult than they had imagined and returned to Europe within a year. The fourth laboured on alone until April 1863, when he was joined by Charles New, a devout young volunteer to the missionary service who had survived a train crash in the summer of 1862 and thereupon decided that a life thus spared should be devoted to God's work.

While in Zanzibar awaiting transport to Mombasa, New had met the Baron Carl Claus von der Decken, recently returned from Kilimanjaro and that 'opportune' fall of snow. In what may have been his customarily impetuous fashion, New immediately resolved to visit the mountain at the first opportunity. However, circumstances postponed the fulfilment of his resolve for nearly ten years, by which time his experience of the 'pestiferous' coast had added a touch of realistic enquiry to his ambition. If Europeans are to civilize Africa, New observed, then some of them must stay alive, and the alpine altitudes of Kilimanjaro seemed to offer more hope of this than the coast.

New reached the foothills of the mountain in July 1871 and though enchanted by the landscape and its prospects, he was sorely harassed by Mandara, the ruler of the Moshi district. Rapacious, unpredictable, usually hindering, but occasionally helpful, Mandara required more 'presents' than New had intended to offer before allowing the young man to attempt an ascent of the mountain. On the first attempt bad weather forced New and his party to turn back before they had even left the forest. But on the second attempt, late in August 1871, New managed to reach the snowline: '. . . The third day we started again, but in half an hour the men complained of benumbed feet and hands. In an hour we came to a stand; the Chaggas said they dared not go any further. I left them, going forward with only Tofiki for a companion. Tofiki did very well for the first one and a half hours, when he sank, scarcely able to speak. He bid me go on — that he would wait there for me, and die if I did not return to him. I went on, reached the snow; I found it lying on ledges of rock in masses, like large sleeping sheep . . .'

As reported to the Royal Geographical Society and in the *Alpine Journal* (above), New's ascent marked the first time a man reached the snow. His reports lack detail, but it seems most likely that he reached an altitude of just over 4,000 metres at a point where the snow extended particularly far down the mountain.

But while he explored the mountain New does not seem to have investigated the idea of a European settlement on its healthy alpine slopes. He returned to Kilimanjaro in 1875, possibly with such an investigation in mind but — in the event — with disastrous consequences. On this occasion Mandara took virtually everything the missionary possessed and allowed him nothing in return. Dispirited, New had no alternative but to turn back. He was ill and poorly equipped when he left Mandara's village, and died before he could reach Mombasa.

Charles New was the only white man to visit Kilimanjaro in the course of the 1870s; Baron von der Decken and his companions had been the only white visitors during the 1860s. For nearly twenty years the mountain attracted very little attention. This hiatus was undoubtedly associated with the declining interest East Africa held for geographic exploration once the riddle of the Nile and the interior lakes had been solved, to the satisfaction of most, by the journeys of Speke and Grant, Baker and Livingstone. But as the explorers moved on to other undiscovered countries, the exploiters stood poised to extend European influence along the trails that now lay open to them.

Of course, the Arabs had been exploiting the resources of East Africa for centuries and it was Europe's determination to end one particularly distasteful Arab exploit — the slave trade — that set the pattern of the European exploitation that followed. Although international legislation had reduced the slave trade to a fraction of its former volume by the mid-nineteenth century, isolated pockets of the trade still flourished. Particularly in East Africa, where the purely Arab trade in slaves for domestic use along the coast, or for export in Arab vessels to Arab and Asiatic destinations, was looked upon as a necessary evil for the time being, to be contained while trade elsewhere was abolished. But though contained, this trade inevitably supplied unscrupulous non-Arab demand too. French sugar planters in the Indian Ocean, for instance, availed themselves of the East African slave trade. A euphemistic nicety termed the Free Labour Emigration System provided their loophole through the agreements to which France was signatory. Beginning in 1843, the System allowed Frenchmen to buy slaves along the coast, set them free and then immediately engage them as 'voluntary' labour for the sugar islands. In 1854 the Portuguese allowed the System to be extended to Mozambique.

The System may have eased a troubled conscience — if any existed — among the planters; and international diplomacy may have been forced to move slowly in banning the Arab trade, but both these acts served only to perpetuate a brisk trade in human beings from the African interior. Through the 1850s, '60s and into the '70s the terror continued. Slave-raiding caravans led by Arab merchants, guarded by armed men and up to a thousand strong still wound their way inland — with the scarlet flag of the Sultan of Zanzibar flying at their head. The principal routes ran from Kilwa and Bagamoyo to Lake Nyasa and Lake Tanganyika (and it was to keep the trade from European eyes that explorers were subjected to such difficulties on those routes to the interior).

Slaves were acquired wherever available on the outward and return journeys. A man wandering alone near his village would be kidnapped; chiefs would be incited to raid rival villages with the aid of the slavers' men and arms. Of the surviving inhabitants the old and ill — the non-saleable — would be abandoned while their homes were burned, their stock dispersed, their crops destroyed. The slavers wreaked havoc on the country and left fear and mistrust among the villages they had not yet attacked.

And the routes to the coast were marked with the remains of slaves who died on the way. An 1871 committee on slavery was told that four or five died for every slave who reached Zanzibar. The coastward journey from the lakes often lasted three months. The slaves were roped or chained from neck to neck, their hands were bound, sometimes they were gagged. Any that died were cut loose, those ill or too exhausted to continue were killed or left to die. 'One woman, who was unable to carry both her load and young child, had the child taken from her and saw its brains dashed out on a stone.' The planters and the politicians saw none of this, and left to them the trade might have continued even longer than it did, but the public in Britain and Europe were incensed by the reports of one man who in his solitary journeys through Africa saw more of the slave trade than any other white man — David Livingstone.

Livingstone's work in Africa, his disappearance and subsequent discovery by Stanley ('Dr Livingstone, I presume'), his reports, his diaries and finally his death in 1873 at a remote inland place, all served immeasurably to hasten the end of the slave trade. 'This will have been something to have lived for,' he wrote. 'If my disclosures should lead to the suppression of the slave trade, I shall regard that as a greater matter by far than the discovery of all the Nile sources together . . .'

But suppression was a slow and tedious process. The British Government, through whom the Arab slave trade could be affected, had long viewed coercion as the best means of achieving abolition. Britain established a diplomatic mission to Zanzibar in 1841 and, with some success, gradually 'persuaded' the Sultan to restrict the trade from his African dominions. By the late 1860s, however, Livingstone's reports, in particular, had inspired a demand for more than just restriction. In 1871 a Government Select Committee called for the total abolition of the Arab slave trade, and finally, in 1875, the Sultan signed such an agreement under the threat of a naval blockade of Zanzibar. There was sporadic smuggling thereafter, and slaves from the Sudan and northern equatorial Africa still reached Arabia via the Red Sea, but by 1880 the slave trade in East Africa was all but dead.

But, in the way of human affairs, the slave trade had not been killed simply by the demands of philanthropic Europe so much as it had been replaced by trade in more acceptable commodities. With the industrialization of Europe, and the opening of the Suez Canal in 1869, Arab traders found lucrative markets for African produce. Ivory and cloves were in constant demand; during the 1870s their significance and value was gradually overtaken by a new development — india rubber. Copra (coconut husks from which oil is extracted), hides, dyestuffs, spices and grain were also exported. In short, as the slave trade dwindled other trade burgeoned. Zanzibar became a centre of respectable economic activity. A regular monthly steamship service was inaugurated in 1872 by the British India Company; a proper Post Office was established in 1878 and in 1879 a telegraph cable connection linked Zanzibar directly to Europe.

Meanwhile, the first steps were taken in Europe's economic exploitation of East Africa. In 1876 William Mackinnon, the founder of the British India Company, and his partners began construction of a road from Dar es Salaam to the interior. Four years later it was over a hundred kilometres long — though it never achieved either its destination or the impetus to trade that Mackinnon had expected. In 1877 British capitalists were invited to formulate proposals for the 'development and civilization' of East Africa by the Sultan of Zanzibar, who had realized that he lacked the resources to fulfil these inevitable and essential undertakings himself. Mackinnon and his associates proposed a grand scheme: a concession wherein his company would build roads, railways and administrative centres throughout the country in exchange for the exclusive right to exploit its resources. They would govern the country, the Sultan would cede all personal authority on the mainland in return for shares in the company and a guarantee that his annual income would not fall below £100,000. General Gordon was invited to join the concessionaires. For a time, a proposal that East Africa should become a sort of Protectorate with Gordon as Governor-General ruling on behalf of the Sultan was also current.

But none of the early proposals for a direct commercial or administrative link between East Africa and Britain came to fruition. Mainly, it seems, because the British Government wished to avoid becoming too tightly bound to the future of the country and the capitalists would not risk their money without Government guarantees. So history meandered on to a conclusion it could have reached much more satisfactorily, and fate took Gordon to Khartoum, where he supervised the collapse of British interests in the Sudan.

Other European powers were interested in the potential of East Africa during this period. Germany had held trade agreements with the Sultan of Zanzibar since 1859. France likewise conducted trade on a regular basis, and a French company once applied (unsuccessfully) for an exclusive ninety-nine year lease to exploit East Africa's resources. And in 1877 King Leopold II set the wheels of Belgian colonial ambition in motion with an expedition to East Africa. Its results were not significant. Subsequently the King applied to the Sultan for permission to lease a tract of coastland where he would found a colony and Belgians would train elephants which, the King believed, might facilitate access to the interior. Permission was refused and ultimately the King's ambitions were fulfilled in West rather than East Africa — on the Congo, courtesy of the Welsh-American explorer Henry Morton Stanley.

But whatever other interest was expressed, or inducements offered, there can be no doubt that the Sultan of Zanzibar would have preferred to commit the future of his dominions to the long term care of the European power he knew best — Britain. The British Government, however, was unwilling to accept the responsibility. In 1881 the Sultan made a will giving Britain control over his succession and, thereby, indirect control over Zanzibar and the mainland from the coast to the lakes. The will asked nothing of Britain but acceptance (and would have become effective in 1888 when the Sultan died), and that undertaking would have pre-empted the claims of other nations and undoubtedly brought a prospect of stability to the region.

But the British Government declined the offer. Because, the Foreign Office explained, acceptance would have contravened the Anglo-French Declaration of 1862, by which the two nations agreed to respect the independence and sovereignty of Zanzibar. Of course, Britain could have persuaded France that the Sultan's will was in Zanzibar's best interest, and new agreements could have been drawn up. But no such attempt was made, and this readiness to decide the future of Africa by reference to the demands of contemporary European diplomacy is symptomatic of colonial attitudes then dominant in Paris, Brussels and Berlin, as well as in London. Increasingly, African territories became the pawns of European power politics, grabbed, carved out and allocated to appease or challenge European alliances with little or no consideration of African interests.

In Zanzibar, however, African interests were the foremost concern of the British Consul, John Kirk, who constantly reminded his government of Britain's responsibilities and of the likely consequences if she refused to accept them. 'We cannot expect to go on for long as we have done,' he cautioned. 'If we hesitate, some other Power, less scrupulous, may step in and forestall us . . . The French priests are very desirous that France should move here . . . The Belgian International Association has ideas that cross the whole continent . . . There are mysterious Germans travelling inland and a German man-of-war is reported on the coast . . .'

Kirk had forged a unique relationship with the Sultan during his sojourn at Zanzibar. He was trusted, and often counselled the Sultan as well as his own Government. Perhaps more than any-one else, Kirk understood the limitations of the Sultan's power on the mainland. He knew that its 'development and civilization' could only be achieved with the involvement of Europe, but believed that this involvement ought to be introduced through the existing power structure — the Sultan's, which it would eventually supersede. And, of course, Kirk believed that Britain was best qualified to take on the job. He vigorously promoted both diplomatic and commercial initiatives. When the Sultan asked for a geologist to investigate an alleged coal deposit on the Rovume Valley, Kirk proposed Joseph Thomson, who had explored the Rufiji Valley a year or two before. Regrettably, the Sultan's expectations of vast mineral wealth were not realized; the 'coal' turned out to be bituminous shale. Thomson found great disfavour at the Sultan's palace as a result, but in London his African exploits earned him an invitation to attempt the first crossing of Masailand, to the north of Kilimanjaro — an expedition intended as much to assess the potential of the country as to describe its geography.

Thomson returned to East Africa in March 1883, and discovered that a German expedition led by Dr Gustav Fischer had recently set off for the interior on a mission similar to his own. From the coast to Kilimanjaro Thomson found himself treading Fischer's footsteps. Both explored the mountain. Thomson made a day trip up to about 2,700 metres, and seems to have had more success in his negotiations with Mandara than many other explorers. He equipped the chief with the tweeds and double-barrelled gun of a country gentleman, and gave him a battery in exchange for the gold watch he had extorted from Charles New nearly ten years before.

Fischer, in his report, observed that the Kilimanjaro region 'seemed well-adapted to European settlement.' Prophetic words. Thomson went on to explore the highlands around Mount Kenya and from there to Lake Victoria; Fischer turned back halfway, and the disparity of the two explorers' achievements undoubtedly contributed to subsequent developments.

Meanwhile, John Kirk had suggested that in view of increasing international interest in the region, Britain ought to sponsor a scientific expedition to collect and describe the flora and fauna of Kilimanjaro. Accordingly, the British Association for the Advancement of Science, the Royal Society, and the Royal Geographical Society pooled their resources and invited Harry Johnston, a twenty-six-year-old naturalist, artist and writer to undertake a six-month study of the mountain. Johnston arrived at Zanzibar in April 1884. While preparing for the expedition he was a guest of John Kirk. Though young, Johnston was not ignorant of travel in Africa. He had explored Tunisia before attaining the age of twenty-one and during 1882 and 1883 had explored Angola and the Congo, where he met Stanley. These exploits, combined with an ebullient, aggrandizing nature, had made a celebrity of Harry Johnston in a very short space of time.

In his autobiography, published late in life, Johnston implies that the primary purpose of his expedition to Kilimanjaro was that of a secret agent, assessing colonial prospects on behalf of the British Government and John Kirk. But while the expedition may not have been quite as innocently scientific as the RGS proposed, there is no evidence in the official archives that it was quite so clandestine as Johnston would have his readers believe. Johnston's claims of political intrigue are most likely an example of the colourful exaggeration he frequently employed.

But there can be no doubt that Johnston had dearly wished he was a secret agent assessing colonial prospects; for, indeed, he behaved just like one. Arriving at Moshi early in May 1884, armed with a letter of introduction from Kirk, Johnston soon negotiated the use of some land from Mandara. Within weeks he had constructed a three-roomed cottage for himself, quarters for his men and a poultry yard; he had sown a kitchen garden with tomatoes, onions, turnips, potatoes, cucumbers and melons from among the seeds he had brought from Europe. He journeyed about the peak, collected assiduously and made copious notes. He had some scrapes and confrontations with Mandara, which subsequently provided the basis of exciting, if largely fictional, articles he sold to the newspapers, while the unembroidered facts were committed to his diary. And among these facts, on 10th July 1884, he wrote: 'I have now taken two decided steps towards the colonization of Kilimanjaro.'

The first of these steps was a request sent to Zanzibar for forty more men and many more trade goods. The second was a letter to Lord Edmond Fitzmaurice at the Foreign Office in London: '. . . Here is a country as large as Switzerland, enjoying a singularly fertile soil and healthy climate, capable of producing every vegetable production of the tropical and temperate zones,' he wrote. 'Within a few years it must be either English, French or German . . . I am on the spot, the first in the field, and able to make Kilimanjaro as completely English as Ceylon . . . for a cost not exceeding £5,000. I have only to invite a certain number of chosen colonists . . . to occupy the beautiful sites which will be given them gratis . . . to cultivate the vine . . . coffee . . . sugar, rice, wheat . . . A road to the coast . . . trade . . . an agreement with Mandara . . .' And so on. Johnston's letter was comprehensive in vision if a little vague on detail. It concluded: 'Here amid my natural history and anthropological studies I shall await inactive until I receive the reply with which I hope you will favour me . . .'

Johnston was never favoured with a reply, but he was not inactive. He signed an agreement with Mandara formalizing his occupation of the land at Moshi, drew up similar agreements with two other chiefs on Kilimanjaro and on 27th September acquired absolute rights over six square miles (fifteen square kilometres) of uninhabited forest near Taveta, in exchange for '300 yards of assorted cloth and thirty-five pounds of beads'. In October Johnston attempted to scale Kilimanjaro. He claims to have reached an altitude of 16,315 feet (4,944 metres) before conditions forced a retreat, but his claim has been questioned.

Late in October Johnston moved to his concession at Taveta. In the forest, work had already begun on the construction of buildings and the cultivation of wheat and coffee. His men had even captured a number of young ostriches for experimental domestication. But there was no letter from London, nor even a word from Kirk in Zanzibar. Johnston waited a week or two longer, then left the concession in the care of four men and set out for Zanzibar, where he arrived in mid-November and promptly boarded the monthly mail boat to England. Before leaving Zanzibar Johnston was interviewed by Kirk, who had no official comment on the Kilimanjaro scheme to convey but wanted first-hand information of it for a report that London had requested.

Given the substance of the proposals and schemes that the British Government had declined during the preceding decades, Johnston's scheme for a Kilimanjaro colony might not have aroused much more than a smile under normal circumstances. But it had arrived in London at a time when the Government's colonial policy had become a particularly sensitive issue — mainly because of Bismarck, Germany's 'Iron Chancellor'.

Bismarck had once declared that Germany would never adopt a colonial policy while he was Chancellor but, by the early 1880s, his countrymen had become most anxious to extend the Imperial German Empire abroad. Apart from the usual aspirations of the business community, prestige and national pride were involved in the ambition. If Britain and France had colonies, then so should Germany, the strongest nation in Europe. And if Germany was the strongest nation in Europe, then she should be strongest at sea too. Colonies would develop shipping, and sea power would follow.

The colonial theme was expounded in the German press and universities. Associations and societies were formed to consolidate and exploit the growing public demand. Early in 1884 Dr Carl Peters, a fervent twenty-eight-year-old enthusiast, founded the *Gesellschaft für Deutsche Kolonisation* (GDK) to raise funds for a particularly ambitious scheme he had devised.

In April 1884, suddenly abandoning his non-colonial stance, Bismarck annexed the Cameroons in West Africa, declaring the territory a German colony despite international acknowledgement of Britain's superior interests there. Annexation of Togo and South-West Africa followed within months; northern New Guinea a little later. Germany's entire colonial empire was acquired in just over a year. The acquisitions were of little commercial or strategic value but they must have gratified the German colonialists. Moreover, and perhaps more importantly, Bismarck's sudden change of policy pleased France by annoying Britain and thus adjusted the European alliances to Bismarck's immediate need and favour.

Certainly Britain responded with some disquiet, and Johnston's letter aroused some fear that East Africa would be next in line for German annexation. Though Johnston never received a reply his proposals were the subject of earnest consideration. A flurry of letters and telegrams were despatched to Zanzibar. Kirk was advised that a foreign flag should not be raised on Kilimanjaro to the detriment of British interests. He was instructed to obtain from the Sultan an undertaking that no rights or concessions would be granted to foreign powers without British consent. The Foreign

Office and the members of Gladstone's Government concerned with colonial affairs no doubt felt these measures were adequate. Indeed, they may have feared Gladstone's reaction more than German annexation. And in the event, Gladstone's reaction was not helpful. In a Cabinet meeting held on 14th December 1884 he 'broke out against the proposed annexations in . . . the Kilimanjaro district' and to a colleague he wrote: 'Terribly have I been puzzled and perplexed on finding a group of the soberest men amongst us to have concocted a scheme such as that touching the mountain country behind Zanzibar with an unrememberable name . . . I have asked Granville (Foreign Secretary) whether it may not stand over a while.'

Meanwhile, Dr Carl Peters had set his ambitious scheme in motion. In the autumn of 1884 he and three other young members of the GDK — Count Joachim Pfeil, Dr Carl Juhlke and August Otto — had assumed false names, disguised themselves as mechanics and sailed to Zanzibar on third-class tickets. They arrived on 4th November and crossed to the mainland on the 10th. After an exceptionally swift and purposeful tour of the hinterland which left Otto dead from disease and Pfeil recuperating in some inland village, Peters returned to Zanzibar on 17th December. Among his baggage lay twelve treaties, signed by local chiefs, which granted the GDK exclusive rights to large areas of the mainland (though not including Kilimanjaro). In each treaty the chief concerned specifically denied that the Sultan of Zanzibar had any jurisdiction over the territory ceded to the GDK.

While Juhlke stayed on in East Africa with further annexations in mind, Peters returned to Europe. He reached Berlin early in February 1885 and immediately sought Imperial protection for the GDK's acquisitions which, indeed, would be impossible to exploit without it. The proposal doubtless suited Bismarck's broader scheme and on 3rd March a Charter of Protection was published. Signed by Kaiser Wilhelm, the document acknowledged the validity of the concessions gained by Peters, accepted suzerainty and declared them (and any further acquisitions) to be under the protection of the Imperial German Empire.

The Charter of Protection (which to all intents and purposes set up a German Protectorate on the East African mainland) was announced five weeks after Gordon fell at Khartoum, while Anglo-French relations were deteriorating because of conflicting interests in Egypt. So Britain was not disposed to pick a quarrel with Bismarck. The need of German friendship was more pressing than obligations in East Africa. Gladstone summed up his government's view during a debate on the Foreign Office vote in March 1885: 'If Germany becomes a colonizing power, all I can say is "God speed her".'

In Zanzibar, reaction to the establishment of a German Protectorate on the East African mainland was not quite so complacent, though attitudes in London and Berlin ensured that it developed slowly. Kirk was advised by the German Consul on 3rd March that a Protectorate had been established. He immediately telegraphed London for details of its extent and location. London finally replied on 19th March with just the barest details. But even this information was withheld from the Sultan, who did not learn that some of his dominions had been annexed until 25th April, when newspapers reporting the event arrived from Europe.

The Sultan immediately protested to Berlin that the territories were his, that the chiefs had acted beyond their authority. And then, fearing further annexations, he despatched a party of armed men to establish a Zanzibar protectorate at Kilimanjaro. En route the Sultan's flag was raised at Taita and at villages in between. At Moshi on 21st June twenty-five chiefs (including Mandara) from

Kilimanjaro and neighbouring districts pledged their allegiance to Zanzibar: 'We, the Sultans of Chagga and Kilimanjaro, do . . . swear that we are subjects of his Highness the Sultan of Zanzibar and that we hoist his flag in the towns of our country to prove our loyalty and that we recognize him as our Suzerain.'

On the way back to the coast the Sultan's representatives glimpsed another party, who avoided contact. Subsequently they learned that the secretive group had been led by Dr Carl Juhlke, marching towards Kilimanjaro where, by the end of July, he managed to conclude ten treaties purporting to place under German 'protection' most of the territories which the chiefs had so recently pledged to the Sultan. No doubt the chiefs had extorted handsome payment for agreements they knew to be worthless, regarding Juhlke as a fool to be fleeced. But in Europe their validity was viewed differently and their worth was measured in terms of the alliances between Britain and Germany and France. And without doubt Germany had scored again.

Kirk protested that the Juhlke treaties were 'pure invention', but events had already turned ominous: on 5th August 1885 five German warships cast anchor off Zanzibar. Not to make war, the British Ambassador in Berlin was advised, but 'to bring the Sultan to a more correct bearing.'

The 'correct bearing' that Bismarck required of the Sultan was, of course, correct only in the German view. It concerned a problem obvious to everyone since the start of Germany's East Africa annexation: while Germans could make questionable agreements with chiefs inland, where the Sultan's control was slight, those agreements were inoperable without access to a port, where the Sultan's control was very strong indeed. So Bismarck needed to convince the Sultan of Germany's right to coastal access. Which he proceeded to do by means of Germany's diplomatic advantage in Europe.

A commission, comprising representatives from Britain, France and Germany, was established towards the end of 1885 to define the limits of the Sultan's dominions on the mainland of East Africa. After a journey along the coast and due consideration, the British and French accepted that the Sultan's rule on the coast was total and extended a good way inland. The German representative, however, denied the Sultan's rule inland and also excluded certain portions of the coastline which, coincidentally of course, would have provided direct access to the territories under German 'protection'. The commission's terms of reference required a unanimous report. When it became clear that unanimity was impossible Bismarck proposed a compromise: the commission should report only those aspects upon which its members were in agreement, leaving aspects of disagreement to be settled by discussion between their Governments in Europe.

Lord Kitchener, the British representative, protested vigorously; and the French representative was similarly displeased. But both, to their surprise, were instructed to concur. And thus a report defining the limits of the Sultan's mainland dominions was signed on 9th June 1886. Unanimous by virtue of its omissions, the report defined the Sultan's dominions where agreed but did not say whether or not he controlled the regions that were not mentioned — and these included certain strips of coastland and all the hinterland. The trade-off negotiated between Berlin, London and Paris worked like this: France needed German support for her occupation of the Comoro Islands, a useful staging post on the voyage to her bases on Madagascar. Britain, on the advice of Kitchener, feared that with Bismarck obviously determined to have an East African port by fair means or foul, and with France so strongly positioned in the Indian Ocean, British interests in Zanzibar would be difficult to defend in times of strife. Britain ought to establish a base at Mombasa, Kitchener had proposed. And so strategic considerations finally determined the partition of East Africa. While France was allowed to consolidate her position in the Indian Ocean and Madagascar, Britain moved into Mombasa, and Germany took over Dar es Salaam — the 'Haven of Peace'. The Sultan was left with Zanzibar, Pemba, Mafia, Lamu, a compensatory income and very little else.

And in October 1886, when negotiators met in London and Berlin to define the boundary between the British and German spheres of influence in East Africa, the Germans magnanimously accepted the concession Johnston had gained at Taveta in 1884 as no less valid than the agreements Juhlke had made in 1885. Thus Taveta is in Kenya today, not Tanzania, and the boundary just to the east of Kilimanjaro has a puzzling kink in it. There is a story that the boundary is kinked because Queen Victoria gave Kilimanjaro to her grandson (the future Wilhelm II) as a birthday present when the Kaiser complained that she had two snowy mountains in her part of East Africa while he had none. The gift, the story goes, caused some realignment of the boundary. This hoary old legend, which must have come from some humorist's pen, is often presented as solemn, unquestioned fact; but there is no truth in it.

Initiation

Camp at the foot of Mawenzi from: Across East African Glaciers: The First Ascent of Kilimanjaro, Hans Meyer 1891

It is chilling to reflect upon the enormity of the problems encountered and overcome by the intrepid gentlemen who first explored the interior of Africa. For the modern traveller such reflection can be demoralizing too: it diminishes the validity of every problem and may disqualify a well-earned sense of achievement — it has all been done before, the explorers' exploits proclaim, and under much more trying circumstances. There is only one way to preserve self-respect while journeying in the shadow of those giants, and that is to make heroes — or even gods — of them. They say that imitation is the sincerest form of flattery. Walking in the footsteps of the gentlemen (and first of all one must believe they were gentlemen) who led Europe into Africa is more than imitation or flattery — it is a sort of worship in which every hardship encountered today should be multiplied and imposed upon the memory of those who trod there a hundred years before. And the image of them wrestling with such a load not only inflates their heroic reputations, it also enhances our own puny accomplishments. The more we admire the achievements of those who blazed the route, the more justified our satisfaction seems when we attain a similar end.

Thus, although the problems confronting me hardly matched those met by the nineteenth century travellers, my confidence was bolstered by their precedent as, like some latter day Livingstone, I began negotiations to hire guide and porters for my journey up and around Kilimanjaro. Most visitors to the mountain take the tourist route and are easily accommodated in the five-day package trip at a fixed fee. My unusual requirements provided a rare opportunity for a little exploitation. In the immortal words of S. J. Perelman the locals would have stripped me 'comme un poulet de printemps', given half the chance. And I suspect I gave them not much less than half a chance.

The independent hirer has little bargaining power. It is obvious to all that he cannot abandon the project without greater cost than any his prospective guides and porters may inflict. Furthermore he is bargaining with an experienced and united labour force; they are all in cahoots, and speak glibly of more generous clients in the past who have given tips far in excess of the total fees now being negotiated. And there are hidden factors unveiled to compound the result of the financial equation just when its primary elements have been agreed. Once convinced that a certain number of men will be required for a specified number of days, for example, one might discover that the individual daily fee is somewhat higher than supposed.

Of course agreements have been negotiated before, and the Park authorities thoughtfully publish the figures, but inflation negates their relevance before they are even printed. Nonetheless, the figures are posted at Park HQ alongside the warnings of mountain sickness and pulmonary œdema.

Differentials and job demarcation, the stumbling blocks of many an industrial dispute, also affect labour on Kilimanjaro, where they are related to status and carrying capacity. Guides earn more than porters and they do not have to carry anything more than their own equipment. But sometimes a guide will share the client's load, his willingness being unpredictably related to the gratuitous generosity of said client that the guide expects to enjoy. These considerations, if left unheeded, may lead the guide/client relationship into a maze as difficult to negotiate as that at Hampton Court, but the promise of a pair of trousers will give the client a head's start at the outset. The addition of a shirt might keep him in front throughout.

Porters do not carry more than fifteen kilos, including their own equipment and provisions, which in effect means that for every two porters hired to carry a client's gear, a third is needed to carry for the other two porters; but since he can only carry fifteen kilos including his own necessities, hiring a third porter may mean that a fourth is thereby required. And so on. I hired four porters for part of my excursion on Kilimanjaro. The fourth man's name was Stephen, or so the other three told me. I never met Stephen himself. Our gear seemed to arrive at each campsite without his assistance and I am not aware that he ever spent a night with us. I was assured that he was engaged elsewhere on tasks essential to the success of my journey, but I occasionally wondered whether Stephen actually existed. I was particularly aggrieved when he failed to collect his pay in person at the end of the trip. The others took it for him. They also collected his tip.

But while negotiations for guide and porters, number of days and daily fees are conducted astutely by the men seeking employment, the prospective employer can feel little incentive to drive a hard bargain. The fees are not excessive by European standards — an average of rather less than four pounds per day per man — and there is no joy in haggling over five shillings with a man to whom it means so much. Better to acknowledge our common ground as soon as pride permits — I wanted to climb the mountain, he needed a little more money to take me there.

Most of the Marangu Hotel's guests set off for the mountain by minibus. After a leisurely breakfast they gather on the lawn that occupies the space between the kitchen and the dining room. Lederhosen and alpine boots, jeans and tennis shoes — an imaginative variety of clothing is often manifest. Age and language may be diverse too; in fact, a camera round the neck and the intent to climb Kilimanjaro are about the only dependable common characteristics. The vehicles carry the guests to the Park gate, from where they begin the five-day eighty-kilometre trek to the peak and back. My trek was to begin at Mweka, forty kilometres to the west along the southern flank of the mountain. We drove there in a Landrover belonging to the National Park, driven by a National Park employee on his day off (it was a Sunday). The vehicle hire charge was considerably below the advertised rate, presumably because accounting procedures had been simplified on this occasion — the official who arranged the hire did not offer a receipt as he stuffed the cash in his pocket.

From the main road and the grassland at the base of the mountain we drove up to Mweka village, through the coffee plantations and past the small holdings where bananas and beans conceal mud-walled houses. Above the village the road was rough and badly pitted, not much used by motor traffic but crowded this morning with people walking down to church. We stopped to buy some more matches and a bar of soap at the last shop. We crossed a broken bridge on the assurance of a small boy that vehicles frequently did, although our driver was certain the remaining logs would break beneath the Landrover and tip us all in the river. As the track became more precipitous, so its surface deteriorated further. The driver became concerned for his sump and the fuel tank. We entered the forest. The track, now just a rough logging track, was overgrown and we halted in a small clearing where there was still room to turn the vehicle around.

We clambered out and three of us — Samja the guide, Francis the porter, and I — took our rucksacks. The driver's friend lounged against the car and lit a cigarette, two young boys appeared and each took a banana from the small bunch tied to my pack. As we were about to leave the driver fell to his knees — but only to examine the fuel tank, which appeared to have sprung a leak. His friend wondered whether they could still get back to Marangu by two o'clock, the two small boys wandered away. There was no ceremony attached to our departure, I felt an uneasy mixture of anti-climax and apprehension as I turned with Samja and Francis on to the track that led to the forest, to the moorland, to the glaciers and the peak. My pack seemed exceptionally heavy and I wondered how wise I had been to hire just one porter for this part of the trip rather than two — or perhaps even three or four.

We began walking at 11.30, about 1,700 metres above sea level. The track soon became a footpath winding between the trees, over fallen logs and alongside the firm deep furrows dug by landowners to carry water from the high permanent streams to their smallholdings far below. The Mweka route, as this track to the peak is known, is not much used. It is marked only by splashes of red paint on some trees, a dull echo of the brilliant red gladioli that grow among them. To European eyes accustomed to the order of forests that have been used and carefully managed for centuries, a tropical rain forest at first seems wastefully untidy. There are dead trees lying about all over the place, fine timber rotting away. Clumps of saplings, thin and whippy as radio aerials, compete for light and air. Different species of tree stand one beside another, vines and creepers lace them together and weave the undergrowth into thickets where you need the help of a good panga (machete) to pass through. The ground cover is close to absolute, only the trails show bare earth and they are kept open by the antelope and cats who occasionally leave their tracks there.

The forest is damp, warm, still: but although there is so much dead vegetation it is a fecund rather than a fetid place. Tropical forests manifest a natural order far more productive than any that man could impose. Nothing is wasted. Every dead thing sustains a host of other organisms. And if you stand alone for a while in the depths of such a place, and let the silence and the moist air envelope you, you may sense the continuity and resilience of the natural processes that actually govern life on earth. All the plant forms around you existed more than one million years ago. A million years, and looking at a tropical forest then and now no man could say that a second had passed.

The track was often slippery, often blocked by fallen, moss-covered trees. As we climbed higher I sensed the altitude and consequent falling temperature mainly in the nose — exertion heated the body but the cold air hit the nostrils. The vegetation changed with the altitude. Certain shrubs were encountered, persisted for a few hundred metres and then disappeared. For a while we passed through patches of richly scented flowers, puzzlingly reminiscent of some known but indefinable perfume. The rich green mosses which had festooned the trees lower down in the forest conceded their position, as we ascended, to long strands of grey lichen, wrapped around the branches like tattered laundry.

It was a humid day, hot and unrelieved by even the slightest breeze. Sweat soaked my clothes and after a few hours my thigh muscles began to cramp up severely. We ate some salt at the next rest (every hour we stopped for ten minutes); the others were sweating just as much as I and Samja even said that he was finding the climb very hard indeed, though I suspect this was more a gesture of commiseration than an accurate assessment of his condition. Francis volunteered little information. He had removed his shirt, but retained his beret. He smoked a cigarette at each rest but drank little of the water we offered. Samja did not smoke, apparently he never has.

We left the forest at about five o'clock. The large trees and dense vegetation ended quite suddenly and we moved on to a grassy sward studded with shrubby heather the height of a man. Samja said the hut where we would spend the night was just ten minutes on, but if he had said it was an hour away the time would have made no difference. I had a severe headache now — it was firmly rooted above and behind my right eye and made thumping excursions into the rest of my brain whenever I turned my head, lifted a foot or, in fact, whenever I did anything other than stand perfectly still.

This is 'overdo', I thought, remembering the Park's warning poster; an open invitation to mountain sickness and pulmonary œdema. But I didn't feel ill. I felt very little other than my headache, my cramped thighs and the absolute futile, pointless stupidity of my circumstances. What on earth was I doing there? I thought, and in what seemed like a flash of genius at the time, I decided that the degree of exhaustion probably can be measured very accurately by how unnecessary it seems. Mine seemed totally unnecessary.

Then we arrived at the hut, one of those circular aluminium affairs built of prefabricated panels, 3,100 metres above sea level, about 1,500 above the clearing where we left the vehicle five and a quarter hours before. While I lay on the grass beside the hut, anxious only that the extensive recuperation my body required should begin as soon as possible, Samja and Francis seemed to wake up. Having discarded their packs they appeared to have as much energy in reserve as men who have just returned from posting a letter. They bounced, I swear, as one set off to gather firewood and the other clambered down to the stream for water. They made sweet, strong tea, with dried milk, sugar and leaves all stewed together over the fire.

The infusion helped a great deal. After that we prepared dinner. I had brought individual freeze-dried meals, each no larger than a packet of cigarettes, each enough for one substantial portion and each comprising either a down-to-earth 'farmhouse stew' or a more exotic 'chicken oriental'. These meals weighed little, took up very little room, could be supplemented with dried beans or peas, and enhanced with herbs, spices, a little curry powder, or perhaps a dash of paprika. Yes, they had many advantages. In fact the only discernible drawback was their dreadful and undisguisable freeze-dried, artificially preserved taste; after my experience on Kilimanjaro I do not suppose that I shall ever be able to countenance it again. At the Mweka Hut, however, I was still very proud of my convenient pre-packaged junk food. As it absorbed water and swelled up in my pot over the fire I spoke enthusiastically of its attributes. The others listened courteously but declined the invitation to sample the concoction. Meanwhile Francis began frying some fresh meat (they had stopped at the market that morning) and a little onion together in their pan. Samja set rice to cook. When the meat was done and the onion nicely browned they added a chopped chilli, salt, and a handful of fresh spinach. They left the mixture to stew for a while before they combined it with the rice and ate. It smelled delicious.

We were asleep by eight that evening, and did not rise until seven next morning, when my thermometer showed one degree centigrade in the hut. Outside, the tussock grass was rimed with frost. The ridge we had to climb that morning was still in shadow but the sun had already cast a pale orange tinge across the snow-covered peak that loomed above it. Kilimanjaro. The sky behind the snow took on a deeper blue as the sun rose. The scene had a transitory air — colour, light and shade changed by the minute — but the peak looked very substantial. We could not see the slopes below the snow; the summit seemed to sit square on the ridge just a few hours away, but was in fact at least two days distant. Beside me, gazing at the magnificent mountain that was such a commonplace thing in his life, Samja remarked: 'It always looks much closer than it really is.'

On the Mweka route the Kilimanjaro moorland begins just above the hut in which we had spent the night. The heather zone ends as abruptly as the forest a few hundred metres below and is succeeded by a rising landscape of low scrubby vegetation studded with boulders and rocky outcrops. Moorland. Coarse grass and a few species of everlasting flower predominate. Colours are muted: grey rock and grey-brown soil, dry grass, sage-green shrubs washed with a silver sheen when the wind turns their leaves to catch the sun. The everlasting flowers have petals like old parchment; some are tinged pale pink but none are as brightly coloured as those that florists in Europe sell.

We had to climb to the brow of the long ridge above the hut that morning; from there we would turn west and begin our stroll around the peak. The brow was at 4,000 metres, just 900 metres and five kilometres from the hut according to the map. But the length of time it would take to get there proved to be a more pertinent measure of its proximity. Samja said at least three hours; in the event if took three and three-quarter hours.

The explorer Wilfred Thesiger once remarked that he found seventy strides per minute a most comfortable pace while travelling with the Bedu. Along London pavements he progresses at about ninety paces per minute. Wilfred Thesiger is an exceptionally tall and lean man with a stride to match, consequently his ninety or seventy strides per minute represent a challenging standard against which to measure one's own ambulatory progress. Towards the conclusion of my preparations for the Kilimanjaro jaunt I was delighted to discover that I could maintain over a hundred paces per minute quite easily during long early morning walks in Richmond Park. On selected parts of the route the rate occasionally touched 120. Since hearing of Thesiger's remark, counting paces per minute has become a feature of every long walk that I make. It can be a diverting habit, like the calculations of speed and distance one makes during a long car journey. But on a mountain the results can be less gratifying, especially at high altitudes, across easy terrain up a gentle incline you would hardly notice at sea level.

Sixty paces a minute was about the most I could manage with any consistency on the Kilimanjaro moorland. And since each pace covered little more than half a metre, we took nearly four hours to walk just five kilometres up 900 metres. The experience was exasperating as much as it was exhausting, probably because ascending a gentle slope at over 3,000 metres is one of those rare occasions when the inability to move faster is not a direct result of physical limitations in the body, but rather an indirect result of limitations in the circumstances surrounding it. The body needs oxygen to produce energy, but oxygen is limited, so you do not tire out muscles so much as you simply lack the energy to use them. 'Do not overdo,' the posters exhort. I should have thought that 'overdo' is virtually impossible.

The broad Kilimanjaro moorlands are well covered with scrubby vegetation, but animals are rarely seen. I saw one or two klipspringers (small antelopes) but leopard droppings were the most frequently encountered evidence of animate life. Being primarily the hair of the leopard's prey they decay very slowly; some are fresher than others of course, but most look like extrusions from a well-used horsehair mattress littered about the mountain.

Samja told me that since Kilimanjaro became a National Park in 1977, the stricter control of illegal hunting on the mountain has encouraged not only leopards, but also lions and wild dogs to seek their prey on the upper slopes. The guides and porters are understandably fearful of encountering these creatures. In 1979 a guide by the name of David was set upon by a pack of wild dogs on the moorland above Mandara Hut. Though no larger than Dalmatians, wild dogs customarily bring down wildebeest and zebra. They are formidable, frightening beasts for whom a man is easy prey. They attack in turns, from all sides; once stationary and surrounded the victim cannot escape. For a time it will stand as though in a trance while flesh is torn away and the entrails exposed. Eventually it will fall, and die while the dogs calmly nuzzle out the liver. A ghastly death to contemplate. David was alone when he met the dogs. He shouted and gesticulated but they still came on. In the first fray one dog took the little finger clean off his right hand. He was saved from further dismemberment by the fortuitous arrival of a large group of tourists upon the scene.

On the moorland, where there is so little evidence of animate life, it requires a conscious effort of mind to appreciate that the environment presents a threat to life, though it is certainly responsible for the death and disappearance of visitors from time to time. In 1977 two brothers failed to return from an attempt to climb the mountain by a south-western route; they were the only sons of a Danish family. The National Park rescue team scoured the area for three weeks. They found a dead elephant at 4,400 metres and a crate of whisky with a parachute attached at 5,000 metres, but no sign of the boys. In 1978 their parents searched again, with twenty-eight guides and rangers from the Park, but to no avail. The fate of their bodies can only be surmised, but the boys almost certainly died of exposure. By all accounts they were not adequately dressed or equipped for the expedition and the mountain is cruel when the weather turns bad. Another lad, similarly ill-prepared, was found huddled and frozen in the lee of a boulder, where he had died while peeling an orange.

By the time we reached the brow of the ridge cloud had enveloped the peak and the wind had turned very cold indeed. Sweat produced during the last hour soon chilled when we stopped. We all added extra layers of warmth and sought a sheltered place to rest among the boulders, though these were small and scattered. The ground was bare on the brow itself and there was little vegetation anywhere else. Nothing much grows up there, just some sparse grasses and a few straggling everlasting flowers. The rock was flat, tabular and cleanly broken — recent sharp breaks, like quarry waste — with none of the comforting eroded roundness usually associated with old rock. It was a bleak landscape, with little comfort of any sort. The air was noticeably thin, movement seemed ponderous, fingers would not operate with quite the dexterity one expected of them. But perhaps this was the effect of a stiff morning's walk, I thought, as I tediously unwrapped a toffee. Or else it was the cold; gloves were essential now.

From the Mweka ridge our route around the mountain followed the contours between 4,000 and 4,250 metres, in and out of the valleys, a scramble rather than a walk or a climb. Fortunately though, the mysterious process of acclimatization began to have a noticeable effect. The headache thumped a little less severely. Legs seemed to function better, breathing matched stride most satisfactorily. Confidence that the undertaking lay within the realms of possibility perhaps was not misplaced after all. The Karanja Valley seemed a reasonable target for the day. It was only two and a half kilometres from the ridge; even so, we took one and a half hours to get there, and it began to rain.

The Karanja Valley is narrow, steep and exquisite. At its head stand the precipitous rock and glaciers of Kibo's southern face, where the Karanja River has its source. Being relatively sheltered and well-watered the valley supports a good growth of vegetation. Moorland vegetation in the main, but dominated by strange varieties the plants we call lobelia and groundsel have evolved in response to the demands of that environment. The lobelias are thick, phallic, metre-high columns of tightly packed leaves, each leaf protecting a small blue flower. The groundsels look like great grotesque candelabra, three metres or more high, with three or four thick branches protruding from the rough stem; each branch crowned with a tuft of leaves. Most of these plants stand alone, but some are lined along the cliff like latecomers at a full theatre.

We camped in the open on a small level patch beside the stream. The rain ceased, but for a while swirling mist and hail threatened an even more uncomfortable night. By late afternoon, however, the sky began to clear. The cloud drifted from the peak, and the valley rim cut a sharp indigo silhouette against the snow and the blue sky. The temperature fell sharply as night approached; by five it stood at one degree centigrade. I did not enjoy my freeze-dried chicken oriental very much, even with added curry powder and peas. Francis made a very large fire and brought in sufficient wood (the trunks of dead groundsel) to keep it burning all night. Apart from the matter of warmth, he was concerned that without a fire wild dogs or a leopard might find our sleeping forms appetizingly attractive. We cut and spread bundles of everlasting flower plants to lie upon, removed only our boots and donned balaclavas when we retreated to our sleeping bags.

The peak was completely clear by then. I lay on my side, gazing at the hard black and white shapes of mountain, snow and sky. There was no moon that night, but the Milky Way was visible — a plume of stars arched from the peak like spray blown from a white wave top. Samja pointed out a satellite. We saw three before we slept and I was reminded of the astronauts, and the time they explored a little of the moon in their Moonrover. On the morning after the announcement of that remarkable event I met Robert, who worked on the coffee farm where I then lived. In distinctive, but very precise English, Robert told me that in Banana Hill the night before men had said that some Americans had just flown to the moon. Very wonderful. But could it be true, he asked, that they had taken a Landrover with them, and were on safari up there?

The fire burned through the night, but by morning our sleeping bags were frozen on the outside and not much warmer inside. It was a bright clear morning, but Samja feared bad weather would catch us en route if we delayed. He expected cloud before noon, and rain — or even snow — soon thereafter. We loaded our packs with the sleeping bags still frozen. And they had not thawed when we reached the next night stop — Barranco Hut, perched on the west rim of the huge breach gouged from the southern face of the mountain by some ancient cataclysmic event. The breach is called the Great Barranco; its sides are 300 metres deep, its floor is laced with streams and littered with boulders the size of houses, its head is hard under the glaciers falling directly from Uhuru Peak — the highest point on Kilimanjaro. The glaciers are seen most spectacularly from the Great Barranco: vast sheets of ice, cold crystal ice, draped like an imperious cloak about the hunched shoulder of the mountain; folded, long vertical crevasses; creased, where the ice flow is caught on irregularities of the rock. Black rock — no, not black, but deep rust-red brown rock. The red of the rock is heightened at sunset, so that from the greater distance of the Shira Plateau, where we arrived next day, Kilimanjaro resembles Ayer's Rock with icing.

We spent two nights at Shira, eating sleeping and husbanding our energies for the long haul over the western shoulder and across the northern flank of the mountain. It is not a frequented route, and Samja was not certain of conditions there, nor was he sure we would find any water. The daily strolls promised to be less tiring now, not simply because I was more acclimatized, but also because as Samja and Francis consumed the food their packs had contained, they offered to carry some of the weighty objects from mine. And by now I was eating their food instead of my own. We ate with spoons from the pot in which the rice had cooked. Samja would make three depressions in the rice, equally spaced around the rim of the pot, and Francis would ladle an equal quantity of stew into each. The meat was tough but it kept well in the cold (we ate at it for seven days); the spinach lasted well too. I usually contributed mint cake, or dried fruit, to the meal.

Francis was thirty-three when I climbed with him, a Chagga, born and brought up at Marangu. He was married and had three children, aged six, four and two. He said he would not have any more, with an insistence tacitly suggesting that he had already taken some action to ensure compliance. He owns a small piece of land which he inherited from his father. The land provides space for his home, and a livelihood; Kilimanjaro provides only a supplementary income. He grows coffee, beans, bananas and maize. He has a few sheep, and in 1979 he bought a young heifer for nearly £200. He has no grazing land, so each day he or his wife must collect fodder from the forest reserve, where they may cut grass but not graze animals. In 1981 the heifer will go to the bull, then she will give milk and two years after that Francis hopes to sell the offspring and thus recoup his initial investment. He is a thrifty man; he claims he would rather walk from Marangu to Moshi than pay the six shillings bus fare. But this could be just talk, the distance is forty kilometres. Even so, Francis had not been to Moshi for five months until we stopped there on the way to Mweka.

Samja was thirty-five, from the Mbulu tribe 150 kilometres or so to the west of Kilimanjaro. Three or four generations ago his people probably would have been at odds with the Wachagga, but Samja moved to Marangu some years ago and lives among them peaceably with his wife and four children. Samja is of compact build, agile, and pale-skinned. He has a small productive piece of land but the mountain is his main livelihood, and because of this he is more inclined to speak of his achievements than of his aspirations.

For seven years he has climbed the mountain regularly, up to thirty times a year, by all routes. He has trained in ice and rock climbing under Norwegian instructors. He is a member of the mountain rescue team. Just the week before our journey together he had assisted in the rescue of a young man taken ill amid the ice of the western crater, and that man has good reason to thank Samja and his colleagues that he is still alive.

The man had been one of four who, though well-equipped, were sadly deficient in local knowledge when they attempted to scale the peak via the south-western glaciers without a guide. They approached the mountain via an irregular route, thus avoiding payment of park entrance fees and the small surcharge that entitles visitors to the free services of the rescue team in an emergency. The four were experienced rock and ice climbers and, possibly overestimating their abilities, they set themselves a tough schedule, reaching the western crater rim on the early afternoon of the third day and expecting to climb Uhuru Peak and return to Barranco Hut by nightfall. They were not equipped for an overnight bivouac and carried no extra food. They might have abandoned the plan to climb Uhuru, and might have reached the hut in good time had not one of their members begun to display alarming signs of disability on the upper glacier. At first he was simply exhausted, then he became euphoric and seemed more inclined to dance than to climb. His friends helped him to the crater where one settled down with him in a sheltered spot among the ice while the other two crossed the peak and scrambled down to Kibo Hut for help. It was nightfall before they raised the alarm. The rescue team, including Samja, came up early next morning. By the time they reached the pair who had spent a night in the open at nearly 6,000 metres, the disabled man was very ill indeed. He had to be hauled on ropes up the rock faces which afford access to the shortest route down to Kibo Hut. A helicopter carried him from there to the hospital, where he received treatment for exposure and pulmonary œdema. The rescue operation undoubtedly saved his life, and it cost him over £1,000.

We walked for nine hours the day we tackled the northern flank of the mountain. Our route crossed the western shoulder at about 4,500 metres, at a barren place reminiscent of an abandoned quarry. The rock there had shattered into slabs; in some places it lay neatly, like those short stretches of Roman road one encounters in the Pennines; in other places it was piled in heaps as though bulldozed out of the way. The shale tinkled like shards of glass underfoot. Two butterflies suddenly appeared, valiantly fluttering upward on the wind, but dangerously misguided, for only snow lay ahead of them. Our traverse followed the ripples of the 4,000 metre contour. The valleys are sharper than on the southern side of the mountain, 'V's rather than 'U's, an indication that the glaciers have never extended so far down the mountain on the northern side.

The peak seems to retreat as you cross the north-west ridges, and the ice seemed much farther away. But Kenya was very close. Glistening tin roofs indicated the position of Loitokitok, the border town from where Ernest Hemingway must frequently have gazed up at Kilimanjaro while he was an honorary game warden based there in the early 1950s. I could just make out the line of the Chyulu Hills, from where my wife and I had caught a memorable glimpse of Kilimanjaro in 1976. I could see the Amboseli Swamp, and the lookout hill we used to climb every morning to see where the elephants were. But most of Kenya was obscured by cloud.

Kilimanjaro

At two in the afternoon we found some water in a small swampy patch of ground recently smudged around the edge by buffaloes. It was surprisingly clean. At five we stopped for the night at the foot of a cliff in the shelter of a large overhanging rock. We were all tired, and as we drank tea the rock above assumed alarming proportions. It was split on all sides and hung directly above our prospective sleeping spot. No doubt it had hung thus for hundreds of years, but no energetic imagination was required to perceive the consequences should it fall while we slept beneath it. We would have been squashed flat instantly, and our families would never know what had happened to us, Francis remarked. With some embarrassed laughter, but no dissuasion, we moved into the open.

Francis made a large fire of heather stumps; we ate thin maize meal porridge and then slept close together on a bed of heather. Our sleeping bags were again frozen by morning. We lay with our feet to the east and when we awoke just before sunrise the morning star was shining directly above. Simultaneously, we each asked the others what they called it in their language. I, the Mzungu — the white man — said we called it simply the Morning Star. Samja said that his people, the Mbulu, called it *Isetseir Loa* — the star which holds the sky while the moon is gone and the sun has not yet risen. And Francis said the Chagga called it *Ngatunyi* — the star that guides the nocturnal traveller safely home.

Above: the final stages of the Kilimanjaro ascent winds above Kibo Hut (lower right) at 4,700m

Below: crossing the Saddle between Kibo and Mawenzi peaks

Above: sunrise over the south-western shoulder

Below: bivouac at 4,000m in the Karanja Valley

Right: stars above the summit, a time exposure from the Great Barranco wall

Left: the northern slopes at 4,000m on the Kilimanjaro circuit

Above: Samja

Below: Simon rests on the Saddle at 4,500m

Above: rock wall at 5,500m on the Arrow Glacier route to the summit
Right: crossing the floor of the Great Barranco, heading for the western shoulder

Left: skirting the Rebmann Glacier near the crater rim at 5,700m

Top: approaching the northern glaciers from the crater rim

Above: ascending the western shoulder

Next page: the inner crater of Kilimanjaro. The Ashpit (centre) is 360m across and 120m deep

Previous page: the crumbling face of the northern glaciers

Above: the leopard immortalized by Ernest Hemingway in *The Snows of Kilimanjaro*, photographed in 1926 with nurses from the Lutheran Mission at Marangu

Right: a painted sign once marked where the leopard had died on the crater rim. Both corpse and inscription have disappeared, only the bare zinc remains

Below: view across the crater from Leopard Point

Descending the scree below Gillman's Point on the crater rim

Ascent

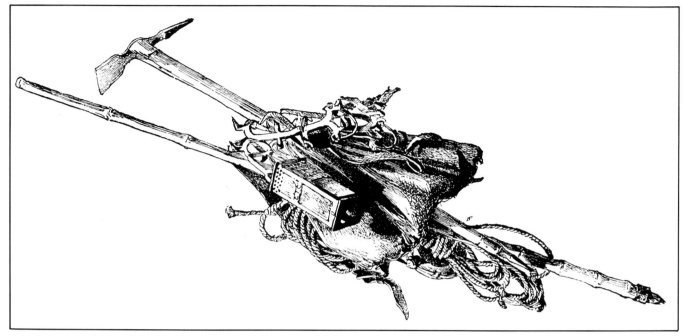

Climbing Tackle from: Across East African Glaciers: The First Ascent of Kilimanjaro, Hans Meyer 1891

The memory of waking up in a frozen sleeping bag with the morning star gleaming above no doubt will persist and mellow with the passing years, but the reality on Kilimanjaro that morning moved swiftly from cocooned warmth to shivering contemplation of an especially arduous day ahead. By quarter past seven we were drinking tea while hill chats, fluffed up like scruffy tennis balls with legs, bounced around the edge of the clearing in search of crumbs. We set off at half past seven, with the temperature still two degrees centigrade below zero.

Samja set a cracking pace. We touched eighty strides a minute in the first half hour and although I was amazed and gratified by my ability to keep up, I soon learned how quickly one person can begin to hate another at 4,000 metres. Samja whistled as he raced ahead and then would stand fidgeting until we caught up with him. Francis maintained his customary position to the rear, and he seemed to be panting too. Each time we caught up with Samja, he would immediately race off again. Whistling. I was reminded of Aesop's tale of the hare and the tortoise, but the memory brought no comfort. I knew only too well that although my plodding progress might get me around the mountain, there was no chance that I would finish in front of Samja. He was in a different league. And I wished he would stop reminding me of the fact. By the time we reached the north-east shoulder and began the long slow slog up to the saddle I was very angry; and Samja was just a small speck among the boulders far ahead when time came for the hourly ten minute rest. I sat down beside a rock, muttering. Francis, manifesting some concern, called loudly to Samja though he was clearly well out of earshot since we had been spared the sound of his piercing whistle for some time. Francis sat down too and accepted a biscuit. I stopped muttering, we discussed the jagged shape of Mawenzi for a few minutes and then recommenced our trek.

About twenty minutes later we reached Samja, perched on a rock in a wide open space just where the route turned sharp right towards Kibo Hut. I stared ahead and marched slowly past in silence, and with as much dignity as I could muster. I was incapable of hurrying past, as might have been more appropriate to my mood. Samja drew up his knees, I recall. He probably laughed. I do now, it's a crazy image: two men at 4,500 metres on a lonely mountain plod arduously across the landscape towards a third man with whom they have been living amicably for several days, and then plod on by without a word. At the time, however, it all seemed very serious and I can still remember the seething anger of the moment. Fortunately the moment passed and normal relations were soon resumed.

But in fact the western end of the Kilimanjaro saddle, that is the final stretch rising gently to the great cone of Kibo, does not seem much related to normality. The landscape is frequently described as a moonscape; 'otherworldly' is another popular description. But the bare brown dusty landscape, littered with boulders grouped like sculpture in a park, is odd and weird by virtue of its associations with this earth rather than its disassociations. If the sea were nearby the saddle would make a respectable beach, at a lower altitude it would conform to everyone's concept of a desert. But at 4,500 metres, in the dry thin air, keening wind and fierce radiant sunshine the saddle, though apparently recognizable, does not fit any known category. The prevailing circumstances of climate and climber's condition are more important than the place. Each man's mountain is his own alone; it's all in the mind, I thought, as I panted up to Kibo Hut. The hut is situated at 4,680 metres. The slope below is just a gentle incline but on Kilimanjaro it reduced me to two paces breathing in, two paces breathing out . . . there was a good rhythm to that, which was comforting until I realized that the phrase *Kyrie eleison* was running through my mind repeatedly, nicely timed to the rhythm of my stride. A useful chant perhaps, but disconcerting to an agnostic seeking not God but just the strength to climb a mountain.

The gentle incline is about two kilometres long, but it took a good hour to climb. Kibo loomed above — not just geographically above the hut we were approaching, but alas, as the next challenge, dauntingly above the effort I was already making. In the crystal clear air, which negates distance, the peak and the ice cliffs at the top seemed huge and very close — yet still so unattainable. And almost beyond belief. It was ironic, I thought, that Africa, the continent of desert, savannah and tropical forest, should be crowned with snow and ice.

In Marangu I had arranged that I would proceed beyond Kibo Hut in the company of another guide, aided by other porters. That I did not climb with Samja and Francis had nothing to do with Samja's race to the saddle; it was simply due to circumstances of time and commitment. Simon was to be my guide to the summit, where we would camp in the crater for as many nights as proved feasible. Equipment and provisions for the crater and the remainder of my safari had been brought to Kibo Hut by three porters — Samuel, Elau and the elusive Stephen. It was arranged that Samuel would ferry gear to and from the crater while Simon and I stayed there alone. The point on the crater rim directly above Kibo Hut is called Gillman's Point and stands 5,650 metres above sea level. The actual summit of Kilimanjaro, called Uhuru Peak, is 200 metres higher and another one and a half kilometres around the rim. Not much further, one might think, but many people find the climb to Gillman's Point quite enough of an achievement.

Gillman's Point is 960 metres above Kibo Hut, that is almost the equivalent of three Empire State Buildings standing one on top of another. The horizontal distance between Kibo Hut and Gillman's Point is roughly 3,000 metres, so the gradient averages about 1:3.3 and the distance covered on the way up is about 3,300 metres — the equivalent of nine Empire State Buildings laid end to end up the incline. The climb is not difficult in mountaineering terms; you could say it is equivalent to scrambling up a staircase rather more than three kilometres long. Or you could say it is equivalent to clambering up the side of nine Empire State Buildings laid end to end at about sixteen degrees. But then at 4,710 metres, where the final ascent of Kilimanjaro begins, there is little more than half the density of oxygen which occurs on Manhattan or at the foot of most staircases. So, in effect, the aspiring climber attempts the equivalent of those feats with the equivalent of only one lung. The result is agonizing, there is no other word for it.

The first explorers of the region had found the forest and moorland altitudes on Kilimanjaro difficult enough, as we have seen, but the cone of Kibo has always been the greatest obstacle to its conquest — and always will be. In 1884 Harry Johnston turned back just above the base of it, at 16,315 feet (4,944 metres), he claimed. In June 1887 Count Samuel Teleki (en route to his discovery of Lakes Rudolf and Stephanie in northern Kenya) turned back at 17,387 feet (5,269 metres), exhausted, with lips bleeding freely and a 'rushing noise in his head'. In the same year a geologist, Dr Hans Meyer, and his companion Herr von Eberstein were defeated by ice and snow at 18,400 feet (5,575 metres). In 1899 a Mr Ehlers claimed to have reached the summit and left his visiting card in a tin box there as proof, but subsequently he was required to modify the claim and admit that it was fanciful, if not deliberately misleading.

Hans Meyer tackled the mountain again in 1889, this time in the company of Ludwig Purtscheller, a highly experienced alpine mountaineer; and this time he succeeded. Meyer and Purtscheller reached the highest point of Kilimanjaro on 5th October 1889 and named it Kaiser Wilhelm Spitze. Hans Meyer was the first man to scale Kilimanjaro and the prospect of being the first surely must have provided considerable incentive for success. I may have been the millionth to climb the mountain, and I know that my commitments spurred me on. I am not at all sure that I would have succeeded without the obligation (of this book for example) to do so, and I want to record here and now my boundless admiration for all those people who climb Kilimanjaro simply for the fun of it, or just because it is there.

Simon overslept on the morning we climbed the cone. We had agreed to leave at four; I woke him at five and I think he had hoped I would sleep longer. There was a three-quarter moon above us; it was a clear, calm and crisp night and the temperature was two degrees centigrade below zero. The beginning of our climb was slow and very quiet; a gentle crunching under foot — the shale was compacted by frost — and an extremely leisurely pace. Samuel carried my rucksack on his head in preference to his back, and Simon carried a large bundle containing tent and sleeping bags likewise. I carried only a small rucksack with cameras, water bottle and mint cake, and I felt quite unreasonably strong. Euphoric, uplifted.

Our pace was between forty and forty-five strides per minute. We stopped after one hour. A quarter way, said Simon, which deflated my self-assurance a little. An hour later we stopped again, at a cave where Teleki had rested in 1887. A piece of galvanized zinc, presumably once fixed to the rock, bore the remnants of a text in English and Swahili telling of the Count's ascent. The zigzags begin just above the cave, where the slope becomes surprisingly severe, and both Simon and

Samuel displayed remarkable agility with the bundles on their heads. We stopped again after three-quarters of an hour, and after that we stopped very frequently. The sun was well up, it was warmer, and cloud had begun to gather over the forest and the moorland below, and around the peak of Mawenzi. The view was spectacular — bird's eye in scope but difficult to enjoy without the benefit of wings.

The pace remained between forty and forty-five strides to the minute, but the strides hardly merited the title any more, though each of them now required a breath. I stopped noting halts and counting paces after about three and a half hours and recall very little of the final stages. I remember encountering some snow, and I remember thinking that the tatty assortment of flags marking Gillman's Point ought to be on the Point, not twenty feet below. I had taken five and a half hours to reach the crater rim and the climb left me devoid of all sensation except a compelling tiredness. There was no sense of achievement, no exhilaration, no energy, no enthusiasm to do anything, no desire for anything except a lot more oxygen. I stretched out in a warm sheltered spot, put my hat over my face and fell asleep.

Simon woke me with a shout from his resting place. Where did I want to make camp? he asked. And I am sure he was aware that, confronting the imminent fulfilment of my ambition, I realized now why Simon had never been especially keen to sleep in the crater. The bleak forbidding terrain did not promise a good night's rest, but there was no alternative. It is impossible for all but the exceptionally endowed to climb the mountain, explore the crater and descend to Kibo Hut in a day. Lesser mortals such as myself must either content themselves with the climb alone, or they must be prepared to sleep in the crater. Simon had acknowledged the good sense of the latter conclusion, but he had not welcomed the prospect with any enthusiasm.

The crater is an almost perfect circle two and a half kilometres across. Its wall is about 180 metres high on the southern side, but rather lower elsewhere; at Gillman's Point it is less than thirty-five metres high. Eccentrically situated within the crater, an inner cone rises to about 5,800 metres — more than 165 metres higher than Gillman's Point and less than sixty metres below the summit itself, Uhuru Peak. Within the cone there is the inner crater with another cone and, in the centre of that minor cone, the ash pit — 360 metres across and 120 metres deep — the core of the mountain. The outer crater is rimmed with spectacular glaciers and ice cliffs. The inner crater is ringed with fumaroles, smoke holes in the ground too hot to touch, emitting heavy fumes and sulphur that coats the slope bright yellow.

In the well-oxygenated comfort of Marangu I had told Simon that following our ascent we ought not to linger at Gillman's Point, but should descend to the crater immediately, press on to the inner crater, establish camp there by lunchtime and complete a short exploration of the immediate surrounding by sunset. The prospect had not seemed unreasonable, and Simon had seemed to agree. We will see, he said. But the reality on the rim was quite different. And when Simon asked where we would camp it was quite clear that he had known it would be. The climb had been more exhausting than anything I had ever known. My headache had returned and I was desperately short of breath. But most disturbing of all I simply lacked the motivation to do anything — there seemed no point or purpose. We'll just get down to the crater floor, I said, and make camp at the first convenient spot we come across.

It was about noon when we left Gillman's Point. We moved around the rim a short way to the north, then clambered down beside a block of solid ice about fifteen metres high, and as many broad and long; one of several on the crater floor, the sole remnants of glaciers that had once covered the peak completely. The crater rim was mostly clear of ice and snow at that season, but large tracts of the crater floor were still filled with frozen snow. It contrasted brilliantly with the dark chocolate-brown shale and the royal blue sky. Sunglasses were essential. The wind had risen, but we were sheltered by the crater wall as we tramped around the edge of the icefield below Gillman's Point. We headed north and the sun was comforting on the left shoulder. The surface of the ice field had been riven by sun and wind and frost into regular lines of sharp pinnacles about 300 millimetres high, they do not break easily, your feet catch in them and you are prone to stumble.

Below Leopard Point, about one kilometre from Gillman's Point, stands another large solitary block of ice, surrounded by shale in a clearing of the ice field. We stopped there, mainly because it was time for a rest and the ground was free of snow, but the spot immediately seemed an ideal camping spot. To me at least, I wanted to get the tent up and make tea for Samuel before he began his lonely descent. I got the stove out, but the wind was too strong and somehow I could not seem to organize adequate shelter for it. Simon was slumped against his load, he suggested we should move across the ice field and make camp on the slope up to the inner crater rim but the suggestion did not appeal to me. I barely had strength to cross the ice, never mind make camp on the other side. Simon went to sleep, I continued to struggle with the stove and the wind, but at one o'clock Samuel announced that he would leave without tea and went off with just a handful of raisins. We arranged that he would return two days hence.

Abandoning hope of ever making tea in that exposed place, I decided to erect the tent and selected a spot beside the ice, no less suitable for its pictorial aspect than for the shelter it afforded. For some minutes I wandered about the patch, removing intrusive stones, trying to assess wind direction and the best position for the tent. But these simple matters seemed very difficult to resolve. There was no co-ordination between thought, intent and action; instead they seemed to contradict each other. A stone moved from one place had to be moved again when the tent position was revised minutes later, and then again when I changed my mind once more. In more senses than one I was going round in circles, dragging the tent after me. The wind was chilling and the full glare of the sun dangerously hot. Finally I bundled up the tent as a pillow, lay down on the shale out of the wind and slept.

While I slept on the tent, Simon moved the rest of our gear to the slope directly beneath Leopard Point. When I woke he suggested that the spot he had chosen was more suitable than mine for camping, there being less risk of melt water rising to that height through the shale, he said. So we pitched the tent (not an easy task on loose shale in a high freezing wind at nearly 6,000 metres) where he indicated and then slept inside it. At four o'clock Simon awoke me with the suggestion that I ought to take some pictures since that was the purpose of our camping in such a forsaken place. I took cameras, crawled out and trudged around the ice block and down the slope towards another great block standing beside Hans Meyer Notch, where the explorer had gained access. Because of the crater wall surrounding us, the view was limited to the ice and shale of the crater itself. A bleak prospect. Melt water streamed from the ice field and froze wherever its motion was halted by a rock or a natural dam of shale. The air was so clear that shadows were sharp, black and forbidding and not diffused to the slightest degree. The sky was darker than seemed natural. And the sun already was low, its imminent departure distinctly hostile with the wind so cold and unremitting.

I was back at the tent by five and the sun set below the crater rim soon after. We made tea; the stove worked quite well in the tent alcove which we had succeeded in aligning downwind. We cooked up a packet of farmhouse stew with added green beans and crawled into our sleeping bags, ready to sleep again by six. The temperature was below zero centigrade and falling. The wind shook the tent vigorously and did not abate all night. Sleep was patchy, shallow and mixed with weird dreams. I wore my balaclava. Occasionally it twisted across my mouth as I slept and I would awaken out of breath, with a sudden panic fear of suffocation. Sharp movement produced a piercing headache and in the dark even raising my head produced a brilliant white ring behind each eye, like a large pair of glasses. Once this occurred in a dream that had me falling from the pavement to escape an assailant who was attacking me in Church Road, Richmond on a night when all the lights were out. As I fell I shouted and the rings flashed behind my eyes. The cry woke me, but whether or not it woke Simon I do not know; in any event he did not respond.

Occasionally, though, Simon did call. John, you sleeping? he would ask. Though more experienced on the mountain, I suspect he was no more comfortable than I at night in the crater. Several times each night I heard him assembling a cigarette, delicately stroking the match head against the friction pad before committing the ultimate stroke (the only way to ensure a flame from those particular matches). There was a flare of light, a few satisfied puffs and then, John, you sleeping? I never did discover exactly what he was smoking; it certainly was not ordinary cigarettes because he had told me that his supply was finished the day before. Perhaps it was loose tobacco from his pockets. It might have been virtually anything combustible — when we finally reached Uhuru Peak he managed to derive quite obvious satisfaction from a cigarette he manufactured from half a page of my notebook rolled around a quantity of frayed brown paper.

The rocks began to split around midnight. I suppose the cold had reached a critical point by then, but I must confess that although I was interested enough to check the watch on my wrist I was not inclined to check the thermometer which was further away and not luminous. Some of the splitting rocks sounded like pistol shots, others broke with a deep reverberation that actually shook the ground beneath us, like a door slammed some distance away in the same building. The ice cracked too, creating visions that pieces from the block nearby might fall on us. Later there were cracking sounds beside my head as the water froze in my water bottle and in the pot we had left standing on the stove.

These sounds and images awoke me repeatedly, and each time revived my awareness of the wind, of the cold, of breathlessness whenever I moved, and of white flashing headaches whenever I moved too suddenly. Morning was a relief, not from tiredness or lethargy — if anything, they were increased — but simply from the night. At sunrise the temperature inside the tent was eight degrees centigrade below zero. We breakfasted on granola and tea, then set off for a short tour of the inner crater.

The wind had dropped (and Simon said that if it had not he would have insisted that we descend that day); it was a beautiful morning. With cameras about my neck I might have been a tourist whiling away the hours between breakfast and lunch, though conditions up there were more arduous than tourists usually encounter and the scenery was awesome.

There is nothing gentle or comfortable about the crater of Kilimanjaro. It, and the material it comprises, is hard and sharp without any edges rounded or softened by wind and sand and water. Instead the rock has been splintered by heat and cold and every piece — whether large enough to be called a boulder, or small enough to be shale — is jagged and sharp. Whole boulders stand split into a dozen or more pieces by the moisture that freezes each night in the fissures. Eventually they will fall apart; if you sit on them the process may be hastened.

We took an hour to climb the 1,500 metre slope to the rim of the inner cone; and another half an hour from there to the rim of the ash pit — a big hole, but not conspicuously containing ash. Large boulders littered the bottom and the sides were composed of shale. Simon suggested I might like to descend the pit, although in Marangu he had demanded an absolute assurance that I would not attempt to do any such thing. But of course he knew that once there I would have no wish to go down. I had a plan of the route, and it did seem feasible (even without ropes) to traverse the upper slope to the column and from there reach the gully leading to the bottom. But once 120 metres down into the heart of Kilimanjaro, where would I find the energy to climb out again? We moved on.

The slopes of the inner crater wall (fifteen to twenty metres high) are patched with reds and browns and bright yellow deposits of pure sulphur; smoke puffs intermittently from holes in the sulphur and the smell is pervasive. Clouds began to loom over the crater, rising and disappearing with amazing speed — as though in a time-lapse film which condenses an hour into a minute. The wind had increased but in the crater we were still sheltered. We walked around the rim of the ash pit towards the terrace on the western crater wall where the sulphur was most prominent. Large lumps lay at the foot of the slope. As we climbed our feet sank in several inches, the ground was very hot and unpleasant fumes rose from our footprints.

Around noon we rested and ate some dried apricots, then we scrambled up the western wall of the inner crater and I stood and gazed in awe at the Great Northern Glacier, vanishing and reappearing among the cloud blowing in from the north-east. The glacier covers the northern summit of Kilimanjaro in a series of terraces, the edges of each fluted into pillars and buttresses as though by design rather than by any natural effect. The ice is pale green where the light passes through, glistening where the sun is melting it; rippled, smooth and shining. Fearfully beautiful, standing with cliffs thirty metres high on the coarse dark chocolate-brown shale.

Descending along the southern face of the glacier towards our camp, we came upon a single slab of ice, perhaps three metres square and 300 millimetres or so thick, standing on edge with no more than a metre of its base actually in contact with the ground. It was about six metres from the face of the glacier; presumably it had broken away some time before (testimony to the assertion that the Kilimanjaro glaciers are retreating). Wind and sun had honed a fine edge on all sides; the sun shone through. Standing free like that it made a magnificent piece of abstract sculpture. Simon was strongly tempted to push it over, but he moved on while I lingered to take pictures.

Clouds and patches of deep blue sky created intriguing shapes and patterns with the ice. Breasting a ridge, two huge buttresses emerged from a bank of cloud, catching the sun like great silver sails. I caught a glimpse of Simon crossing the ice field about a kilometre ahead and turned in that direction, then I vomited, violently but completely without warning. 'Overdo,' I thought, watching the liquid soak away from the bright orange pieces of apricot. The subsequent heaves produced only liquid and then I felt stronger. But if this is 'overdo', I wondered, reviewing the meagre accomplishments of the morning, how can I possibly do less. I reached the camp around half past one. Simon had already taken his sleeping bag from the tent and was stretched out in a sunny sheltered niche. I made some black very sweet tea and stretched out inside the tent. The sun was wonderfully warm through the fabric, I put my hat over my face and slept from two till four.

We were camped under Leopard Point, as I have said, but although the name was familiar enough to him, Simon had never heard the legend that Ernest Hemingway had immortalized in *The Snows of Kilimanjaro*. And when I explained that sometime in the 1920s the frozen corpse of a leopard had been discovered on the rocks above us, Simon expressed incredulity. Why would it have climbed up there? he asked. And when I told him I intended to climb up and look for the remains of the creature, he expressed amusement. If a cow had been left there only seven years before, did I expect there would be any recognizable remains of it there now? he asked.

Nonetheless I climbed up and scoured not just Leopard Point but the entire ridge from Gillman's Point to Hans Meyer Notch. I found three rusty cans containing paraffin cached among the rocks and, on a level space under the highest rocks of Leopard Point, a tea-tray-sized piece of galvanized zinc. Nothing was written on it, though a hole in the centre suggested that it had once been fixed to something and perhaps had carried a message. Probably it had marked the spot where the leopard had been found once the creature itself had disappeared entirely. There is ample proof of the leopard's existence to be found in photographs and published reports of the day, some of which suggest the manner of its disappearance. Dr Reusch, the local missionary who first discovered the relic, once cut off an ear as a souvenir. He would have preferred to take the entire head, he wrote, but found the corpse too dry and frozen for easy dismemberment.

'No one has explained what the leopard was seeking at that altitude,' wrote Hemingway. No, but whatever ambition had driven the creature to such a lifeless landscape of shale and ice, I thought while sitting there, it had found a primeval place beyond which no living thing can proceed.

The sun had a ring around it just before it set that evening. There was no mellowing of evening, the sun simply disappeared abruptly below the crater rim and the cold intensified sharply. We heated up a chicken oriental, but only Simon ate, while I vomited not long after he had finished. I blamed the smell of the freeze-dried concoction as much as 'overdo' for my condition, but Simon was concerned. He squeezed my sides as I retched and wanted to know if I was ill or just sick. It took me a little while to understand what he meant: was I vomiting from nausea or was I ill with something more serious. No, I told him, I was just sick; and crawled into my sleeping bag more concerned with the problem of getting out again in a hurry should I feel nauseous than with any threat of pulmonary œdema.

The second night was calm, which was a blessing, but very cold again. The condensation from our breath froze on the inside of the tent; and the spittle that sometimes dribbles from the corner of your mouth while sleeping froze on my makeshift pillow. Sleep was easier without the wind, though still disturbed by flashes of white behind the eyes whenever I turned abruptly and still distinguished by nightmarish dreams. In one I found myself taking a lift to a flat where a group of women I have known were gathered. Two of them were kissing passionately, one was declared to be eight and a half months pregnant, though it was not obvious. I was naked, so were they, but their behaviour soon made it clear that this was not an orgy, but a sacrifice. And I woke up just as I realized who was the intended victim.

We left the tent at about eight the next morning — the time is not exact because by then my self-winding watch had run down and frequently stopped during the long hours I was prone and immobile. The sun was encouragingly warm, there was no wind, and so we would tackle Uhuru Peak. We did not discuss the route. I did not particularly want to take the tourist route, which would have meant clambering up to Gillman's Point and following the crater rim from there, but I preferred to leave the matter to Simon. We crossed the ice field directly in front of the tent and moved around the slope of the inner cone towards the south-west. We would not take the tourist route, it seemed, though the alternative was still unclear. When we stopped for a rest on the hour we were directly beneath Uhuru Peak, about 250 metres below the summit and 500 metres across the ice from the foot of the incline. We could either continue a kilometre or so to the south-west and climb up behind a buttress to approach Uhuru Peak from the west, I thought, or else we could cross the ice field again and climb the rim to join the tourist route about half way between Gillman's Point and the peak. The former seemed more challenging and the latter more likely. Okay? asked Simon, and set off to the south-west, following the edge of the ice field. We would climb behind the buttress, I deduced, which became an increasingly daunting prospect the closer we approached. Shit, said Simon a little later, when we were opposite the scree and rock behind the buttress. Too hard, he said, and the rock near the top too dangerous. So we crossed the ice field and tracked back to the east again. Under Uhuru Peak we scrambled up a fifteen metre ridge expecting, presumably, to find a gully or passage of some sort leading to the peak. There was none and we had to descend again.

Across that part of the ice field, boulders and patches of shale had melted clear of the ice, blotching the surface like islands. The eastern crater rim stood in hard silhouette, the sun not yet high enough to light the inner wall. Light cloud wavered about the rim, varying the depth of blue in strong but repetitive compositions of sky, rock and ice. Photographs of the crater comprise very little else, I thought with some mortification.

Halfway back to Gillman's Point, at a spot we could have reached with relative ease two hours before, we climbed the scree and joined the tourist route to Uhuru Peak. The final climb around the rim crosses several ridges before you see the bundle of flags and sticks that marks the summit, and even then it is still about 500 metres away. The southern glacier falls away to the left, cloud blanketed most of the country below, though we could see distant mountains far off to the south. My pace slowed to thirty-eight strides a minute, each required a full breath and none carried me more than a boot length forward. The gradient was slight, but at 5,860 metres only downhill is easy. I reached the summit at quarter past eleven on Friday 29th August 1980, according to my watch. Simon and I shook hands, took some pictures of each other and ate a little mint cake. How odd, I thought, that we should be so high above every one of all the millions of people then standing on the continent of Africa.

Snow and Ice

Kilima-njaro seen from above Moshi from: The Kilima-njaro Expedition, H. H. Johnston 1886

My ascent of Kilimanjaro had taken eight days, and the subsequent descent occupied another four. Reaching Uhuru Peak undoubtedly was the culmination of the experience, but I must confess that I found Uhuru Peak an anti-climax. I stood on the summit, with Africa and much of the world at my feet. I recall a sense of relief, but none of achievement. On reflection, the leopard I did not find, the ash pit I did not descend and the first glimpse of the ice cliffs which is so durably printed in my mind, but which I could not capture on film, all impressed me more deeply than those moments at the summit.

Some weeks later I climbed to the crater again, hoping that it would be easier to take the photographs I wanted on a second visit. It was a more extravagant expedition than the first. With Samja, Francis and two porters, I started from the Shira Plateau; we traversed the southern flank of the mountain and climbed to the rim via the steep and arduous Mweka route. We spent two days and one night in the crater before descending via the Arrow Glacier. It was easier to take photographs in the crater on the second visit, but the magic had gone. The special affinity I felt for the place was rooted in the experience of the first visit — a unique experience that is easy enough to remember but can never be repeated. I concluded the ascents should be left unique; there is little point in climbing to the summit of the same mountain twice.

But descents are another matter. Indeed, an attraction of mountain climbing that should never be under-estimated is that once you reach the top the trip is all downhill. Every descent is an exhilarating leap back from painful achievement to the comfort of a familiar world. It would be nice if there could be more of them.

I climbed to the summit twice during the time that I spent in the Kilimanjaro region, but I made a number of other journeys to the upper slopes and thus managed to descend the mountain several times. In all I spent thirty-five days on its slopes, and between times I spent many hours reading about the nature of the mountain and the life it supports. My trips up the mountain usually had some end in mind — some place or thing that I wanted to see, or photograph, or find out about — but my descents were more in the way of pleasant rambles through landscapes that I was beginning to know very well. And as my knowledge of Kilimanjaro increased, my interests were increasingly concerned with the mountain itself, rather than with my experience on it. The remaining chapters will reflect this change of viewpoint. They are, in effect, the record of a descent from summit to rain forest, but they concentrate on the mountain, its history, and the phenomena — some commonplace, some unique — that are encountered on its slopes.

There can be no doubt that a high mountain is an excellent place from which to contemplate the world and its phenomena. And Kilimanjaro is rather better suited to this purpose than most mountains because its mass, standing alone and rising to 5,700 metres from a plain just 750 metres above sea level, forms one grand ecosystem within which lies an example of virtually every environment on earth. From waterless desert to tropical rain forest. From glacial ice field to sweeping savannah. It has been said that the descent from summit to rain forest on Kilimanjaro is akin to travelling from the Arctic to the equator.

The icy dome which caps Kilimanjaro was once thought to be the source of the rivers that support so many people around the foot of the mountain. Now, however, it is known that by far the greater part of the river flow derives from the forest and moorland. Very little comes from the ice. Not least because there is very little precipitation up there. While lower altitudes enjoy up to 2,000 mm of rain a year on average, the summit and the crater probably receive little more than 125 mm. And that, of course, falls as snow.

Snow. I remember standing at the window in winter as a child, waiting for flakes to stick to the pane so that I could look at them through a magnifying glass. I wish someone had suggested that I should put a black cloth outside for a minute or two, which was how the physicist Robert Hooke had collected specimens for a paper on snow flakes he read before the Royal Society in 1665. Hooke was a pioneer of the microscope, and his paper — illustrated with woodcuts of his observations — was the first to examine the structure of snowflakes in detail, although their form had been noted by the Chinese nearly 2,000 years before. Water congeals into flowers, declares one ancient Chinese text. And the flowers of water are always six-pointed, observes another, while the flowers of plants are five-pointed. Glaciers were another phenomenon which was slow to engage the enquiring minds of Europe. The term, French in origin, did not enter the English language until 1744 according to the Oxford English Dictionary, although the German word — *gletscher* — was communicated to the Royal Society over one hundred years earlier. As the oldest scientific body in the world, the Royal Society was the recipient of many quaint and curious observations while science was still in its infancy. And in 1669 its Fellows were informed of the 'Icy and Chrystallin Mountains of Helvetia, call'd the Gletscher'. Helvetia is the original name of Switzerland and a traveller reported to the Society that the highest mountains of that land are always covered with snow. And the snow, he continued, 'is hardened into Ice, which little by little . . . itself turns into a Stone, not yielding in hardness and clearness to Chrystall. Such Stones closely joyned and compacted compose a whole Mountain, and that a very firm one . . .'

The idea that glaciers are actually flowing rivers of ice developed very slowly, and their fundamental role in the creation of the European and North American landscapes was not fully explained until the 1840s. And even then the explanation was not generally accepted. In 1849, when Rebmann made his controversial observations of snow on Kilimanjaro, there were still some authorities who contested the suggestion that valleys could be gouged out by glaciers, and that glacial debris could account for several puzzles of geology.

The main reason for their objection to the new theories was, by and large, a preference for the old explanations. And these, of course, attributed all natural phenomena — puzzling or otherwise — to the work of God. For such gentlemen science was little more than a new means of substantiating (or even explaining) the teachings of the Bible. So that when enquiring minds began to remark how odd it was that huge granite boulders should litter the valleys of limestone mountains (in the Jura for example) when the nearest source of granite was over a hundred kilometres away, the old school chose to interpret the phenomenon as conclusive proof that the Flood which so beset Noah must have been very severe indeed to be capable of washing boulders about so lightly.

For supporters of the new scientific dogma, however, such explanations were too simplistic. They believed there must be a natural law governing every event and phenomenon; and while perhaps willing to concede that everything was ultimately attributable to God, they wished to discover and define the laws by which the wonders of the world had been created. And in this respect the Flood was a very poor explanation of granite boulders in limestone valleys. No great perspicacity was needed to observe that large boulders do not travel easily on water, and are unlikely to be washed over intervening mountain tops or distributed so extensively by the movement of water alone. Some other explanation must be found. For quite some time, though, the early scientists could do little more than document the phenomenon. They collected observations which must perforce await a convincing theory to explain them. And Charles Darwin brought a worldwide dimension to the puzzle when he observed anomalous 'rivers of stone' in the Falkland Islands during his voyage in the *Beagle.*

Theory finally caught up with observation in 1840, though proposals close to the truth had been put forward before then. The Scottish geologist James Hutton, for example, in 1795 published his *Theory of the Earth* which contained the suggestion that large masses of rock could have been moved by glaciers, which he called 'those rivers of ice which are formed in the highest valleys of the Alps'.

Hutton's ideas were developed and vigorously promoted in the early 1800s by John Playfair; they were also substantiated in Switzerland — quite independently — by Jean Perraudin who in 1815 tried to interest academics in his idea that both the anomalous boulders and the scarred rock faces he noticed in the alpine valleys could be the result of glacial movement in earlier times. But Perraudin was a peasant farmer and Hutton was a thinker ahead of his time. Perraudin lacked clout and Hutton lacked evidence, so the ideas of neither received the attention they deserved. Thereafter several authorities lent support to the glacial theory — Goethe and Darwin among them — but it was a French geologist, Louis Agassiz who assembled theory and evidence in a form comprehensive enough to give him credit for the whole idea.

Agassiz's theory was published in 1840. His concept of the Ice Ages and of the extent to which glaciers and general erosion have modified the landscape was arguably the most significant addition to our knowledge of the earth since Newton explained gravity. Certainly Agassiz's work was fundamental to the science of geology, inspiring, as it did, the concept of the earth as a dynamic self-perpetuating entity from which continents arise as a result of great internal heat and are subsequently dismantled by the forces of erosion. An infinitely slow but inexorable process in which fire and ice are uniquely complementary.

Fire and ice — volcano and glacier; Kilimanjaro.

Glaciers today cover over 15,000,000 square kilometres of the earth's surface. Of this vast area, 12,000,000 square kilometres are in Antarctica, where the ice is up to two kilometres thick and so heavy that it has depressed the land surface below sea level in many places. By contrast, glaciers cover only about twenty square kilometres of the entire African continent, with just four square kilometres on Mount Kilimanjaro. And the glaciers on Kilimanjaro are, it seems, melting so rapidly that the mountain may be completely bare before very long.

Nowadays it is possible — though perhaps inadvisable — to clamber up the eastern side of Kilimanjaro with the aid of nothing more substantial than a pair of tennis shoes. On the popular routes you need never step on ice and climbing equipment is superfluous. But the ascent was not always so simple. On his first attempt to scale the peak (in July 1887), Hans Meyer and his party encountered snow drifts two metres deep on the southern slopes of the Saddle. The stream known today as Last Water, Meyer dubbed *Schneequelle* — 'snow stream' — because it bubbled from a bank of snow. On Kibo, taking a route very near that by which most climbers ascend the mountain today, Meyer and his companion Eberstein met extensive fields of firn at little more than 4,500 metres. (Firn is snow which has survived at least one melting season; it is unconsolidated but represents the first stage in the formation of a glacier.) Struggling from one field to another in a fog of mist and sleet, Meyer and Eberstein climbed on for three hours. There Eberstein fell exhausted. Meyer went on alone while his companion rested, but not very far. About 150 metres up the snow merged into one continuous sheet. Great blocks of ice lay to the right, just ahead lay a stretch of broken ice and beyond that stood a wall of blue ice, wreathed in sleet and fog, at least thirty metres high and quite impossible to climb even were Eberstein able to assist. Meyer retraced his steps.

From the Saddle the next day, with the aid of binoculars, Meyer estimated that the ice wall he had reached stood just below the crater rim, at an altitude of some 5,500 metres. The ice was continuous over the entire peak, he observed, thickest to the north and most extensive to the south, but at no point could the summit be reached without some strenuous ice climbing.

Meyer returned to Kilimanjaro in September 1889, determined to scale the peak and make a general survey of the mountain. In the light of his previous experience the '89 expedition was most carefully planned, not least in the participation of Ludwig Purtscheller, an alpine guide of considerable renown. A base camp was established on the moorland, via which a series of porters ferried fresh provisions every three days from Marangu to the men tackling the mountain. Meyer had a small tent, a number of camel hair blankets, and two sheepskin sleeping sacks for the advance camps. Technical equipment included theodolite, compasses, aneroid barometer, boiling-point thermometer, photographic apparatus and all the paraphernalia needed for collecting and preserving geological and botanical specimens. Climbing equipment comprised ice axes, manilla rope, warm woollen clothing, snow goggles, sun veils and strong alpine boots. Purtscheller had a pair of crampons too, but Meyer's had been shipped to Ceylon in error.

Given that the ice cliffs on the northern crater rim were so precipitous and the southern glaciers so extensive and fractured, Meyer and Purtscheller concluded that the easiest route to the summit lay across a neck of glacier extending down the south-eastern slope of the mountain. From the Saddle the incline appeared less severe and the ice less fissured at that point. The two men began their assault on the peak from an advance camp at 4,300 metres. They set off at half past two on the morning of 3rd October. By comparison with Meyer's 1887 attempt, conditions were good — the lower slopes were clear of snow and the weather favourable.

Moving up the northern wall of the great valley which sweeps down the south-eastern flank of the mountain, the climbers encountered the first snow an hour after sunrise at about 5,000 metres. By nine o'clock they had reached the lower margin of the solid sheet of ice which then crowned the mountain. As they had deduced, the cliff was neither so high nor so precipitous at that point as elsewhere. Instead of soaring vertically for thirty metres or more, it was a sloping platform affording relatively easy access to the ice dome above. Even so, the slope was never less than thirty-five degrees; it could not be scaled without cutting steps and the ice was extremely hard. Twenty axe strokes were required for each step.

Purtscheller cut the first step at half past ten and two hours later he and Meyer reached the upper limits of the smooth glacier ice at about 5,700 metres. From there on steps were no longer necessary, but progress was no less arduous for all that. The ice was eroded, the surface weathered into grooves and ruts with spikes in between up to two metres high. The two men repeatedly sank to their armpits in snow-filled crevasses; they took nearly two hours to climb the last 150 metres to the crater rim. And when at last they stood on the rim, gazing at the crater that no man had ever seen, they realized that they could not reach the highest point of the mountain that day. It lay a good hundred metres higher and at least an hour and a half to the west. They had neither the strength to get there and back down the mountain before dark, nor the necessities to spend a night at that altitude. So they decided to return to their camp and try again in three days' time.

The two men slept late the next morning, then spent the rest of the day making technical observations, adding to their collections and taking photographs. The following day they moved the advance camp up to 4,600 metres and at three o'clock on the morning of the third day began their second assault on the peak.

With the route clearly marked and the ice-steps still unspoilt they reached the rim in just under six hours. They turned to the west and, troubled only by the weathered surface of the ice, reached the highest point on Kilimanjaro at precisely half past ten, 6th October 1889. Meyer planted a small German flag, shook hands with his companion, led three cheers for the Emperor and named the peak Kaiser Wilhelm's Peak — the highest point in Africa and the German Empire.

Fresh from their success on Kibo, Meyer and Purtscheller tackled Mawenzi a few days later and in three ascents compiled an impressive survey of its major features though they failed to reach the summit. Then they returned to Kibo. On 17th October the two men scaled the northern slope of the peak to about 5,700 metres, where they found the ice wall compact, continuous, between thirty and thirty-five metres high, and quite impossible to climb without extensive resources of equipment and personnel.

On the 19th they tackled the peak from the east, just north of the route on which Meyer had failed in 1887. This time, however, weather and circumstances were much more favourable. Setting out from a cave in which they spent the night at about 4,650 metres, Meyer and Purtscheller reached the edge of the ice cap at 7.30 and were able to gain access to the crater by way of a notch which had been obscured from view on Meyer's previous attempt. Ice-climbing tackle was necessary, for the notch was just a depression in a mass of ice over sixty metres thick, but in little more than an hour the two men were standing on the crater floor at the foot of the eastern wall. Further progress was impossible, however. Meyer would have liked to visit the central cone, less than one and a half kilometres away, but the sheer quantity and fissured nature of the intervening ice made access out of the question in the time available. Ice and snow filled the crater. Meyer noted that the inner walls and the crater floor were almost entirely covered; on the north side huge masses of ice sloped towards the inner cone in a series of great blue and white terraces; another vast ice mass extended towards the cleft in the western wall, through which it fed the glaciers on that side of the mountain. Meyer described the crater and its ice as 'a spectacle of imposing majesty and unapproachable grandeur'.

In 1887 Meyer gained first-hand information of the extent to which ice blanketed Kilimanjaro, with figures, facts and photographs to substantiate his observations. He returned to the mountain in 1898, principally to make a thorough study of the glaciers, and was astonished by the extent to which they had retreated in the meantime. On all sides he found the ice limit about a hundred metres higher than before, but the greatest change was in the crater. The notch (now called Hans Meyer Notch) was twice as large and the ice half as thick. A second notch had developed to the south and the cleft in the western wall, from which ice had cascaded in 1887, was virtually clear. The crater floor was more or less ice free, Meyer reported, with just a few isolated remnants of the former grandeur. A valley had been exposed between the central cone and the northern wall, down which water flowed into the crater from the melting glacier. The ice was still up to sixty metres thick in places, the scene was still impressive — indeed the melting process had created fantastic towers, crevasses, pillars and caves in the ice — but it would not last long, Meyer conjectured. Unless the climate changed, he wrote in 1899, the crater rim soon would be bare rock and in two or three decades Mount Kilimanjaro would be devoid of ice.

Well, the process has not been quite so rapid. Photographs taken in the 1930s show the mountain still well covered, and even in 1981 the ice cap is not unimpressive. But the retreat of the ice is detectable everywhere. The glacier Purtscheller and Meyer climbed so arduously in 1887 (the Ratzel, so named by Meyer in honour of a Professor of Geography at Leipzig University) is now just a narrow strip of terraced ice standing alone on the bare mountain side. The crater rim is entirely free of permanent ice; a sizeable glacier (the Furtwangler Glacier) remains on the south-western crater floor, but to the east and south there are just three or four house-sized blocks of ice; and the upper edge of the northern glacier, which Meyer saw leaning inward from the crater rim, now stands a hundred metres down the outer slope of the mountain.

But why is the ice retreating? You may say it is melted by the equatorial sun, and of course that must be a large part of the explanation, but the story is not quite so simple. In fact the *direct* melting effect of the sun on ice at high altitudes is limited, mainly because flat ice surfaces reflect so much of the sun's radiation. Paradoxically, glacial ice in places like Kilimanjaro melts most readily where it is suitably shaded from the direct rays of the sun and thus able to absorb a greater proportion of radiant energy. This point is eloquently demonstrated by the series of small pits which a scientist found on the south-western glacier in 1957. Just a few inches deep, there was a butterfly at the bottom of each pit and they all had the rough outline of the insect within. Air currents must have drawn the butterflies up the mountain; when they died and fell on the ice their wings reduced reflectivity enough to melt out the pits into which they sank.

But while glistening ice reflects so much of the sun's energy, dull brown lavas absorb a great deal; the ground becomes quite warm, so that where glacial cliffs stand on bare rock or shale, destructive melting occurs at the base. Heat from the ground undercuts the ice; an overhang is created which eventually breaks away and is itself undercut, and so on. It is an accumulative process: as the cliffs break up so more surface becomes susceptible; and where vertical fractures create shade and give passage to warm air, then differential melting occurs in the vertical plane too, creating the towers, columns, pinnacles and fluted surfaces which are such a distinctive feature of the Kilimanjaro glaciers.

Melting by any means destroys glaciers, but an equally crucial factor in the retreat of the glaciers on Kilimanjaro is the failure of the annual wet seasons to replace the ice which melted during the preceding dry seasons. The Saddle probably receives less than 250 millimetres a year on average and precipitation appears to diminish rapidly with altitude above the Saddle. Just 125 millimetres or even less may be the average on the summit. But whether 125 millimetres or 1,250 falls on the summit each year, it is demonstrably not enough to halt the retreat of the glaciers. And never has been enough in the ninety years since Hans Meyer first scaled the peak. Which immediately raises a question: if the ice has been melting steadily for nearly a century when did it accumulate?

A study of Kilimanjaro and its glaciers conducted by geologists from Sheffield University in the 1950s provides an answer. Their work shows that Kilimanjaro has a long history of glacial advance and retreat. Since the mountain attained a height of 5,000 metres over half a million years ago, the periods of volcanic eruption by which it grew from the earth have been interspersed by times when thick ice clothed the peak. Fire and ice. The sequence of eruptions is told in the layers of different lavas which are found around the peak. In some cases the age of the lavas and their eruption can be determined by potassium/argon dating procedures. The glacial sequence is told in the valleys carved through the lavas as the glaciers advanced, and in the moraines left behind as the glaciers retreated. These mingled histories of fire and ice on Mount Kilimanjaro have been carefully disentangled and described by the Sheffield scientists.

In respect of the ice cap they have defined a sequence of eight glaciations. The present ice cap began retreating about 200 years ago, they say, and the most recent glaciation therefore probably coincided with the Little Ice Age which Europe endured between 1400 and 1700 AD, when the Thames froze frequently and Breughel the Elder depicted a severe winter in his painting *Hunters in the Snow*. So the retreat of the Kilimanjaro glaciers supplements the more general observation that the earth's surface has been warming up in the recent past. The evidence of glacial retreats in Europe, for example, and climatic records, show quite clearly that we have been enjoying a particularly warm spell for some time now. Furthermore, estimates of global ice volume suggest that periods as warm as this have occurred only three times in the last million years. The troughs in between are several and severe. They represent the earlier Ice Ages and can be correlated (tentatively, at least) with the advance and retreat of glaciers on Kilimanjaro.

There were times when Kilimanjaro was bare of ice for 10,000, 20,000, perhaps even 100,000 years, though we will never know whether this was due entirely to climatic change or partly due to volcanic activity as well. Obviously every major eruption would have swept the mountain clear — and what a spectacle that must have been — but no matter what removed the ice we can be certain that only a deteriorating climate brought it back. The most severe Kilimanjaro glaciation appears to have occurred from about 70,000 to 10,000 years ago, and could have coincided with the Würm Ice

The inner crater wall, with cloud rising from the north-east

Views of the northern glacier through thickening cloud

Ice cliffs on the northern glaciers

The head of the northern glacier, a panoramic view from the crater rim

Next page: glacier ice cliffs and terraces on the south-eastern slopes of the summit

Compositions of sky, rock and ice: the Kilimanjaro crater icefields

Remnants of the glacial ice sheets that once filled the crater

Glacial remnants. *Above:* free-standing slab was three metres high, 300mm thick

Descent from the summit. Mawenzi in background, Kibo Hut in middle distance

Ages of the northern hemisphere, when ice spread south to the Thames in Europe and to the latitude of Detroit in North America.

On Kilimanjaro at the height of the glacial period an unbroken sheet of ice blanketed the entire mountain down to about 4,000 metres, with many separate glaciers flowing on down to 3,500 and even 3,000 metres (the present tree line). Both Kibo and Mawenzi were completely engulfed, forming centres of dispersal from which ice flowed all over the mountain. A huge glacier from each peak flowed on to the Saddle, so heavy and powerful that they sheered off many of the small volcanic cones which stood in their paths. Eventually these two great rivers of ice collided head-on, and their irresistible progress was diverted to north and south.

Much of Kilimanjaro's spectacular landscape was created during this time when the ice extended well below where the Horombo Hut stands today. I find it awesome to imagine how the mountain must have looked then, and while we may regret the diminishing spectacle of the glaciers perhaps it is as well to remember that their retreat affords a rare view of the crater and the very heart of Kilimanjaro.

Volcano

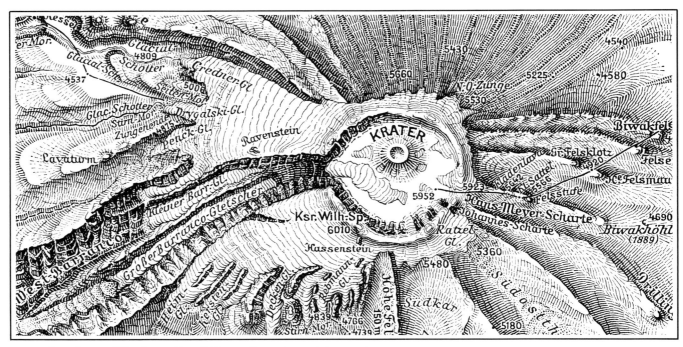

Karte des oberen Kibo from: Der Kilimandjaro, Hans Meyer 1900

The crater of Kilimanjaro is a primeval place and decidedly uncomfortable, yet I was drawn to it. The idea of spending some days and nights in the crater awoke a compelling mixture of reverential fear and wonder; similar, I suspect, to the compulsion which draws some people unquestioningly to church. And like churches, the crater also invite contemplation of the eternal mysteries.

We tend to view the earth principally in terms of the life it does, or does not, support. 'Lifeless' seems the most appropriate description of the Kilimanjaro crater, for instance. Reasonable enough; but the life-oriented view does obscure the phenomenon from which all life developed. Life on earth is no more than a very thin blanket recently wrapped around the globe, and only where it is broken or drawn aside are we exposed to the scale of the mystery that lies beneath. The crater of Kilimanjaro is such a place, introducing a mystery of epic proportions.

No one knows for certain how the earth began. It may have been an aggregation of interstellar dust; it may have been a gas cloud that condensed and solidified. It may even have been a lump of the sun sucked away by the gravity of some large passing body. Nor is it known for certain whether the earth's core is cooling down with the passage of time, or heating up as a result of compression and radioactive decay. But despite this lack of basic knowledge, it is certain that the earth's structural machinery is powered by heat. Heat creates the forces and tensions of which continents, mountains and volcanoes are surface manifestations. And though ponderous, those forces keep the earth in a constant state of flux. The landscape seems stable, but the earth is over 4,000,000,000 years old and on the scale of geological time its surface is as restless as the ocean on the scale of a human lifespan. Every continent ebbs and flows; mountain ranges rise and collapse like waves; volcanoes erupt and die . . .

There are no proven theories to account for the origin of the continents and their associated phenomena. And as though to heighten the mystery, some authorities maintain that we never will possess a set of unyielding universal truths to explain such things. Even so, a recent attempt — the theory of plate tectonics — has an appealing grandeur and simplicity. The theory holds that the earth's crust presently consists of six enormous plates effectively 'floating' on the denser mantle below. The plates move in response to forces emanating from the earth's interior. Where plates collide one is driven beneath the edge of the other; continents rise and buckle on the upper plate, creating mountains like the Rockies and the Himalayas. And in other parts of the globe, where the internal forces cause a plate to break and drift apart, earthquakes accompany the formation of rift valleys, and volcanoes burst through the fractures which develop along the rift margins. The Atlantic Ocean is an example of a rift basin where two plates have been drifting apart for a very long time. The African Rift Valley is an example of a basin just beginning to form. From the Red Sea to the Kalahari, the immense forces below the earth's crust are quite literally ripping Africa apart. And the volcanoes which have erupted along the rift — Kilimanjaro for instance — are tokens of its progress so far.

Like icebergs at sea, volcanoes hide most of their bulk beneath the surface (except that while icebergs reveal about one ninth of themselves, volcanoes show only a hundredth or even a thousandth part). In effect volcanoes are mere pinpricks in the earth's skin, but occasionally they give a potent hint of the tremendous forces contained below. When Krakatoa, an island off Java, erupted in 1883, for example, the explosion was heard by a coast guard 4,750 kilometres away across the Indian Ocean. In South Australia, 3,205 kilometres distant, people reported a series of explosions which sounded like rock-blasting. Over 36,000 people died in the Krakatoa eruption and its aftermath, most of them in the tidal wave which swept the neighbouring coasts of Java and Sumatra. And when it was all over two-thirds of Krakatoa had disappeared. An ocean trough 270 metres deep marked the spot where a volcano 800 metres high had stood. Huge clouds of volcanic dust had been blasted into the atmosphere; the dust soon girdled the earth and two years thereafter exceptionally brilliant and colourful sunsets and sunrises were still commonplace everywhere.

No one could have predicted the scale of the Krakatoa eruption, and although ominous rumblings during the preceding weeks had given some warning it is unlikely that many people moved far enough away to escape the catastrophe. Similarly, in 1902, when Mount Pelee on the Caribbean island of Martinique began to threaten Saint Pierre, a flourishing seaport, more people moved into the city for safety than left it. On 8th May a fireball of super-heated gases and dust burst from the volcano's flank above the city. In just three minutes Saint Pierre was flattened and 30,000 people died. There were two survivors.

More recently, devastating earthquakes in Algeria, Italy and Greece, and the spectacular eruption of Mount St. Helens in America have provided ominous reminders of the ease with which tectonic forces may modify the landscape. These events always occur where the earth's crust is under stress. Mount St. Helens is associated with the San Andreas Fault which one day will topple San Francisco and Los Angeles like a pack of cards. Indeed, St. Helens is but one of nearly 300 active volcanoes which encircle the Pacific Ocean. Another belt of nearly a hundred active volcanoes stretches from

South-East Europe, through Asia and into the East Indies. Down through the Atlantic there are nearly fifty volcanoes; in Africa sixteen, all but three of them directly associated with the Rift Valley. And of course there are many, many more dormant, dying and extinct volcanoes. Kilimanjaro is one of these, though the exact definition of its status was in doubt for some time.

Very few Rift Valley volcanoes have ever erupted cataclysmically, though a lack of records throws doubt on any assertion. There are no reports of volcanic eruptions in any of the sparse Greek, Roman, Arab, Chinese and Portuguese accounts of the region. Indeed the earliest known account of anything that might be called volcanic activity in East Africa is a Chagga folk tale of how Mawenzi acquired its battered appearance. Recorded in 1914 by Bruno Gutmann, a German Lutheran missionary, the tale goes like this: one day Mawenzi's fire went out, so he went to his neighbour Kibo for a hot coal or two. Kibo obliged, and gave Mawenzi some bananas as well. On his way home Mawenzi let the fire go out, so he returned to Kibo who once more obliged with coals and bananas. Again the fire went out, and again Mawenzi returned to his neighbour once more. But this time Kibo did not oblige. Instead he took a stick and beat Mawenzi severely about the head.

Now it has been suggested that this is a folk account of three eruptions on Kibo which occurred after Mawenzi had become extinct but before much erosion had affected the peak. Lavas from the first two eruptions must have nearly reached Mawenzi, the interpretation goes, while the third blast was powerful enough to strip Mawenzi down to the bare rock. Could be. Early residents who observed eruptions may well have handed down this account of the events, though the tale gives no clue as to when they might have occurred. The Chagga have not occupied the region for more than three or four centuries, it is true, and this could imply that Kibo has erupted quite recently, but then again, the Chagga could have heard the tale from people who were on Kilimanjaro before them. Like many folk tales the story of Kibo and Mawenzi is equivocal. It could even be a simple admonition to children who do not look after things they are given.

Written accounts of Kilimanjaro begin in 1848 with its first European visitor, Johann Rebmann, though he makes no comment on the volcanic aspect of the mountain — perhaps wisely, given the uproar which greeted his simple observation that the peak was covered with snow. But of course the volcanic origin of the mountain was quite obvious especially to the experts who followed in Rebmann's footsteps, and no doubt they wondered when it last erupted and whether it was likely to do so again. In 1861 the geologist Richard Thornton noted that Kibo's crater rim was at least still partially intact; in 1886 the naturalist and adventurer Harry Johnston bemoaned the failure of his attempts to gaze 'down into the crater of Kilimanjaro from its snowy rim'; but the first man to achieve any real chance of establishing the volcanic status of the mountain was the first man who succeeded in climbing it — the geologist Hans Meyer. And he, as we have seen, found the crater filled with ice. Well, not *quite* filled . . . It is true that snow and ice prevented him reaching the inner cone rising 150 metres or so from the crater floor, but Meyer did note that the upper part of the cone itself was completely free, which suggested to him that the cone still retained enough of its original heat to prevent any snow accumulating there. But otherwise the volcanic activity of Kilimanjaro was a thing of the past, Meyer concluded in 1889, without any sign of hot springs, fumaroles (secondary vents emitting gases) or solfatara (secondary vents emitting predominantly sulphurous materials).

In Meyer's view Kibo's last major eruption had occurred when the previously rounded dome had collapsed to give the mountain its present truncated appearance. This collapse had created a caldera on the summit (any such large pit-like volcanic depression is more properly known as a caldera — Ngorongoro is an impressive example), in which subsequent minor eruptions had built up the inner cone, though 'apparently without forming a crater', Meyer wrote in 1900.

Meyer's authoritative conclusion that Kilimanjaro was extinct and lacked even a crater prevailed for nearly forty years (though it must be said that less than half a dozen individuals climbed the mountain during that time, and none were able to explore the summit any more fully than Meyer had done). Meanwhile, the ice on the summit continued to diminish; suggesting to some that the mountain was heating up rather than cooling off, but eventually affording access to the inner cone.

The first man to gaze on the inner crater from the rim of the cone was a former officer in the Cossack Army of Imperial Russia, now become a Lutheran missionary, Pastor Richard Reusch. In his long residence at Marangu, Reusch climbed the mountain more than forty times. On his first ascent in September 1926 he found a frozen leopard; on his second, 19th July 1927, he discovered the inner crater. The leopard achieved fame as the introduction to Ernest Hemingway's celebrated *Snows of Kilimanjaro;* Reusch's name was given to the crater he had found. But Reusch does not seem to have been especially impressed with his namesake. The removal of the leopard's ear and a later attempt to behead the relic at least achieve mention in his accounts of those early expeditions — but the inner crater is not mentioned at all.

Nonetheless several climbers visited the Reusch Ash Pit in the years immediately following its discovery, and the first suggestion that Kilimanjaro might not be extinct after all came from the mountaineer H. W. Tilman, who scaled the peak in August 1933 and casually noted in the Kibo Hut book that he had seen sulphur fumes discharging from the outer rim and found lumps of sulphur lying about the crater floor.

Tilman's observations caused some excitement down below. Perhaps the heat allegedly destroying the ice cap was not residual after all, perhaps it was increasing, perhaps the discharges Tilman had seen were the precursors of a major eruption. In search of an answer the good Pastor Reusch climbed the mountain again not three weeks after Tilman's visit. He looked for the sulphur discharges but was unable to confirm Tilman's observations. In fact he specifically denied them. 'I am afraid Mr Tilman must have mistaken a certain kind of whirling little cloud resembling smoke for the sulphur fumes,' he reported.

And with that denial from the man most familiar with the mountain, Tilman's report was rejected and fears of imminent eruption subsided. Until 1942, when in July a visitor once again noted sulphur discharges. This time the observation was checked by a volcanologist, J. J. Richard, who in August 1942 found sulphur gas gushing from several vents, and deposits of very pure sulphur around the holes. The Second World War was in progress at the time, but Richard's report nonetheless created a flurry of concern which extended well beyond the immediate environs of the mountain. 'Kilimanjaro an active volcano,' reported the first of a series of letters to the London *Times.* One correspondent drew attention to the early reports of residual heat. Julian Huxley, the eminent naturalist, remarked that the evidence seemed to indicate a 'recrudescence of volcanic activity' on the mountain. The *Illustrated London News* reviewed the evidence in a story entitled 'Active or Extinct — The Problem of Kilimanjaro', but on the mountain itself the problem by then seemed to be not whether it was active, but when it would erupt.

In February 1943, on his second visit to the crater, Richard found the number of fumaroles increased from six to twenty and fumes detectable at some distance. In July a meteorologist

P. C. Spink found almost continuous parallel lines of fumaroles on the west and south of the crater. Gas emission was copious, Spink reported, the sulphur beds were extensive and he frequently sank to his knees in the warm deposits.

Meanwhile, the residents of west Kilimanjaro reported ominous rumblings from the interior of the mountain, like 'trains coming and going rapidly on an underground railway,' they said. Houses were cracked by tremors which occurred intermittently during the first months of 1944. Fears of an eruption rose. In April 1944 the geologist Peter Kent reviewed the situation in an article published by the prestigious science journal *Nature* under the title 'Kilimanjaro: an Active Volcano'. 'There can be no doubt that the mountain should not be classified as extinct,' wrote Kent. He wondered whether a recurrence of the great eruptions which had smothered parts of East Africa with lava and ash in the past was likely, and concluded that such an event would develop very slowly — if it happened at all.

But sober assessments in scholarly journals were no comfort to people living around the mountain. Ol Doinyo Lengai, a volcano in the adjacent portion of the Rift Valley, had erupted recently, not violently but with enough force to spread clouds of choking dust for miles over the surrounding countryside. Lengai stands in an area inhabited only by nomadic pastoral tribesmen, who were able to move on hurriedly, but the slopes of Kilimanjaro were densely populated. An eruption would threaten thousands. Vast wheat fields, coffee plantations, banana groves and hundreds of smallholdings would be inundated. Amid general concern that something ought to be done, Spink marked out the sulphur beds with stakes so that any increase could be measured; and Richard arranged for an African guide to take monthly temperature readings on selected fumaroles. No one could prevent an eruption if it was destined to occur, but these monitoring arrangements might at least provide some warning. In the event there was no eruption, nor even any increased threat of one.

By the time the War ended in 1945 Richard had noted a striking decrease in activity on the crater. Spink, on the other hand, noted an increase during the same period, but whatever the significance of these conflicting reports, a threat unrealized soon became no threat at all. As months became years and Kilimanjaro remained only mildly active — if not actually extinct — the people living around the mountain relaxed. The scare was over.

But while the population at large learned to live with a warm and gently smoking volcano looming above them, their earlier concern eventually stirred the authorities to action. Government departments examined the evidence and decided that a thorough survey of the mountain should be made to assess not only the threat of eruption, but also the effect of the diminishing ice cap on local water supplies, and the extent of the sulphur deposits in the crater. World shortage had made sulphur a valuable commodity at the time, and the relevant department wanted to know if the Kilimanjaro deposit was worth exploiting.

The survey was undertaken by the combined forces of geologists from the University of Sheffield and the Tanganyika Geological Survey. The first expedition to the mountain took place in 1953; the second in 1957. As regards the threat of eruption, the survey set all minds at rest: Kilimanjaro was dormant and all but extinct. As regards water supply, the survey found that this depends more upon rainfall on the slopes than upon ice on the summit. And as regards sulphur, the investigators found the deposits too small to warrant exploitation; so we were spared the ghastly prospect of a sulphur mine on top of an enchanting mountain. But behind these simple answers lies a wealth of information which in itself provides the fullest possible answer to the simple question you might have asked when you first turned from the summit: why is there a mountain here in the first place?

Of all things on earth mountains are surely the most permanent, but even they rise and fall. Little more than one million years ago, for instance, Kilimanjaro did not exist. A million years is a concept that barely touches human comprehension, but in geological terms it is a relatively brief period, and a substantial mountain born within the last million years is a comparative youngster. Which makes Kilimanjaro particularly interesting, for such youth combined with such bulk indicates that the mountain grew at an exceptional rate.

Before Kilimanjaro, the country now dominated by the mountain was a gently undulating plain between 600 and 900 metres above sea level. Grassland presumably, studded with trees, rimmed by prominences which were ancient even then and are still there today — Namanga, Longido, the Pare Mountains, the Tsavo and the Taita Hills. Where Kilimanjaro now stands a large river is said to have flowed, no doubt attracting to its banks substantial numbers of animals; some strikingly similar to those inhabiting Tanzania's game parks today, some unfamiliar and destined for extinction, and perhaps including some members of the ancestral human population whose remains have been found at Olduvai, on the western edge of the then uninterrupted plain, about 250 kilometres away. Flowing to the sea via the gap between the Pare Mountains and the Taita Hills, the river rose more than 500 kilometres west of Kilimanjaro and along its course drained the Eyasi, Manyara and Natron basins. Nowadays those basins are enclosed by Rift Valley faults and their waters cannot reach the sea, but in ancient times access was unrestricted simply because the Rift Valley itself did not exist.

The African Rift Valley is about 6,400 kilometres long, 50 kilometres wide and varies in depth between about a hundred and a thousand metres. The mechanism of its formation is uncertain but the effect is that of a huge block fallen from an upswelling portion of the earth's crust, rather as the keystone might slip if the curve of a brick-built arch were expanded. And just as adjacent bricks would be loosened when the keystone slipped, so the earth's crust was fractured along the edges of the upper plateau when the central block of the Rift Valley fell. Some of the pressure responsible for the initial upswelling burst through these fractures along the rift margins, some of it escaped within the rift itself, and with the release of pressure quantities of magma (molten rock) rose to the surface from reservoirs thirty to fifty kilometres down in the earth's crust, creating volcanoes.

The East African Rift Valley began to assume its present form over 2,000,000 years ago. There are twenty major volcanic centres in the region — all directly associated with rift faulting and together they form some of the finest volcanic scenery in the world. The caldera at Ngorongoro is twenty kilometres wide, Kilimanjaro rises 5,000 metres above its base, Ol Doinyo Lengai is still active, there are several idyllic crater lakes — overall the region is spattered with literally hundreds of cones and craters. More than 250 of them in the Kilimanjaro complex alone.

The first volcanoes to burst through the basement rock upon which Kilimanjaro now stands were at Ol Molog, Kibongoto and Kilema, each about thirty kilometres from the present day summit and situated to the north-west, south-west and south-east respectively. These eruptions began about one million years ago and gradually built up a complex of peaks and valleys in the form of a ridge running WNW-ESE, about a hundred kilometres long, sixty-five kilometres wide and up to 3,000 metres high. There were a number of outlets involved in the construction of the initial volcanic massif at Kilimanjaro, but about three-quarters of a million years ago activity became concentrated at three main points and the cones of Shira, Kibo and Mawenzi began to take shape. For several hundred thousand years the three cones were puffing away together, each attaining a height of about 4,800 metres, but about half a million years ago Shira began to fade and became totally inactive soon thereafter. Subsequently most of the upper cone of Shira has been removed by erosion, leaving only a remnant of the crater rim and an extensive plateau where the volcano had stood.

For a while, however, Kibo and Mawenzi continued to grow together. Eventually they both stood almost 5,500 metres high, their lavas mingled on the slopes of the massif, their peaks now high enough to accumulate snow. But Mawenzi seems to have died before the first glaciation struck Kilimanjaro and, being higher and steeper than Shira, once dead was subject to more precipitous erosion. At one stage the entire north-east wall of the mountain from 4,000 to 5,500 metres collapsed, releasing the waters of a lake which had formed in the crater and thereby flooding volcanic debris over 1,100 square kilometres of the land lying between Loitokitok and the Chyulu Hills, to the north-east. The collapse created the spectacular gorge whose 300 metre cliffs are such a daunting feature of the peak.

Subsequent erosion has stripped the upper parts of Mawenzi down to a brittle, fractured rock widely interleaved with material from later eruptions forced through then existing fissures to form what geologists call 'dykes'. These dykes, over half a metre thick and rising vertically among the host rocks, are a distinctive feature of Mawenzi. Being of a lava that probably cooled more slowly than the host rock, they are harder, resist erosion longer, and so give the peak its dramatic jagged outline of towers and thin pillars.

Mawenzi presents by far the most dramatic aspect of the Kilimanjaro landscape, and by far the greatest challenge to mountaineers. Several faces on Mawenzi have never been climbed. Some are probably unclimbable. Simply reaching the summit by known routes is extremely difficult and hazardous. The rock is brittle and so fractured that in places the mountain resembles a badly constructed wall — block piled upon block and very likely to fall. Occasionally the blocks do fall; while I was on Kibo, an Austrian climber was killed by a rockfall on Mawenzi. And when I visited the small tarn below the northern face of the peak Simon told me of the fatal accident which had befallen two climbers on the rocks above. The details can never be known but the circumstances in which the bodies were found suggest that the two men — both experienced climbers — had reached the summit successfully by the standard route, but had attempted to pioneer a new descent. One body was found low down the scree. It seemed the man had detached himself from the rope for some reason and then fallen. The body of his companion was found suspended at the end of the rope about a hundred metres above. He too had fallen, but the rope had caught across an overhang and left him dangling some distance from the face, unable to regain the rock or climb up the rope. The body hung in such an inaccessible place that to retrieve it a marksman severed the rope with a bullet.

But while erosion stripped Mawenzi down to a challenging pinnacle (and at 5,120 metres Mawenzi is still the third highest mountain in Africa after Kibo and Mount Kenya), Kibo continued to grow — albeit not so rapidly as before. In all, geologists have identified nine distinct lavas which erupted from Kibo after Mawenzi became extinct. The most extensive eruptions occurred about 360,000 years ago, when lavas welled from the crater on all sides of the cone in broad sheets up to fifteen (and occasionally fifty) metres thick. These lavas filled the Shira calderas to the west, fanned

Kilimanjaro summit at sunset from Shira Plateau

The Inner Crater rim. *Above:* hot smoking fumaroles.
Below: deposits of pure sulphur

Left: stream-bed pool on Shira Plateau
Below: water-worn cobble in dry stream
Above: frost-shattered boulder in the crater
Right: vertical icicle beside Arrow Glacier

Left: Zebra Rock, above Horombo at 3,800m is a low cliff face stained by percolating surface waters
Above: north-eastern Saddle at 4,600m with Kibo slope beyond

Lava boulder containing porphyry crystals above red lichen on slopes of Mawenzi at 4,500m

across the Saddle and around Mawenzi to the east and, at their farthest extended fifty-five kilometres north-west and thirty kilometres south of the Kibo crater. At one time the entire cone and much of the adjacent slopes must have been covered with this lava. Even today, despite subsequent eruptions and erosion, it is still the most distinctive rock encountered on the mountain. Named the rhomb porphyry lava by geologists, the rock is easily recognized as a dark, occasionally vesicular lava studded with crystals of rhombic (and sometimes diamond-shaped) cross section. The crystals are two to five centimetres long, and the peak is littered with examples which have weathered from the parent rock. Searching for a perfect specimen can be an absorbing distraction from the rigours of the climb — obsessively so, since most of the crystals you find are likely to be either broken or worn. I never found a perfect specimen. The crystals are first encountered in the vicinity of the Horombo Hut and here, where the lavas flowed down particularly deep valleys, there is also evidence of extraordinary tunnels left in the lava when the skin solidified while the interior was still molten and thus able to flow away. The roofs collapsed eventually, but the vertical walls up to fifteen metres high are still clearly distinguishable. The stream below Horombo Hut runs between a pair of them.

Kibo attained a maximum height of about 5,900 metres some 450,000 years ago and has been slowly shrinking ever since. The eruptions continued, but intermittently, with long periods of dormancy (up to 100,000 years) in between, when erosion sculpted Kilimanjaro towards the form it presents today. Glaciers smoothed off the Saddle and cut deep valleys in the flanks of the mountain. Sometime around 100,000 years ago a huge landslip from the summit (probably triggered by internal subsidence) breached the south-west crater wall and carried away about a thousand metres of the cone below, thus creating the impressive dimensions of the Kibo Barranco.

And while erosion took its toll, Kibo's eruptions became progressively weaker. There was a time when lava lay in a molten pool across the crater floor, but as activity diminished, so its effects gradually retreated to its source. Subsidence created concentric terraces, upon which the penultimate eruptions constructed concentric cones.

Eventually the magma withdrew down the central vent. Sometime more than 200 years ago a mildly explosive last puff placed a beautifully symmetrical cone of ash around the rim of the vent and, with that, volcanic activity came to an end. In one million years those mysterious forces within the earth had piled four thousand million cubic metres of raw volcanic material above ground.

Life

Great-billed Ravens from: The Kilima-njaro Expedition, H. H. Johnston 1886

The leopard which died on the crater rim is an evocative example of an animal exploring the limits of existence. No warm-blooded creature can live long in such places without some imported means of survival, and the leopard presumably lacked even the strength to regain the slope down which it easily could have reached the safety of the Saddle. Whatever it might have been seeking at that altitude, the leopard — to my mind — will always remain a salutary example of over-zealous ambition. I would have expected a leopard, usually such a sensible animal, to have known better.

Like the wild dogs, for instance, which the explorer Wilfred Thesiger encountered on the summit of Kilimanjaro in 1962. This is a less romantic tale than that of the leopard perhaps, and certainly less well-known, but it is a story of a reconnaissance at the limits of existence rather than of an unsuccessful attempt to cross them.

Thesiger climbed in the company of George Webb and a well-known guide Effata Jonathan on 13th February 1962. They first saw the dogs at about eight o'clock, while resting near Hans Meyer Point en route around the crater rim to Uhuru Peak (then still called Kaiser Wilhelm Spitze). The dogs were unmistakable — round-eared; black coats marked with blotches of brown, yellow and white; inquisitive demeanour. There were five of them standing on the edge of the southern glacier, which then still ran as a continuous wall of ice parallel to the crater rim. As Thesiger, Webb and Jonathan proceeded to the summit, the dogs followed, showing considerable interest in their presence, but keeping to the glacier, parallel and about three hundred metres away. At one point dog

62

tracks to and from the crater crossed the route the three men were taking, indicating not only that the dogs had already explored further afield but also that they were capable of leaving and regaining the southern glacier rim should they so choose. Furthermore, since they generally hunt morning and evening, the dogs were likely to be hungry after their climb. And there was no meat except that which they were following around the crater rim. Discussion as to the likelihood of attack ensued among the three men.

On the plains wild dogs single out a weaker member of the herd, which they corner and kill in the most frightening manner, by dismemberment, often consuming part of the unfortunate animal before the whole is dead. Five dogs against three men on open ground at that altitude probably favoured the dogs, if they were bold enough to attack. And the men saw good reason to suppose that they might as the dogs continued to track them around the rim, displaying all the lively curiosity of their kind and undoubtedly weighing the odds most carefully. At the summit, while the men dug the record book from the snow and ice, the dogs sat on the glacier crest, watching every move. But when the men began their descent the dogs disappeared beyond the glacier crest and were not seen again. Which was a relief to the men, and a sensible decision on the part of the dogs. There is no doubt that they could have inflicted some injury, and they may have brought a man down, but there was also a good chance that one or more of the dogs would have been injured in the fray. And since wild dogs are co-operative animals whose strength lies in numbers, injury to one would have affected all. On balance it was more sensible to suffer their hunger and preserve their numbers for an occasion when the odds promised food without injury.

Similar decisions mark the limits of existence for every organism. Territories are determined in the balance of an innate drive to exploit new pastures against the caution of experience gained in the security of home. New pastures, of course, are colonized by venturesome individuals. Many die, but those possessing the means of survival gain the advantage of space and resources available only to themselves. It was some sort of suitably equipped venturesome bacteria which first extended life's dominion from the sea to the land many, many millions of years ago. Now they are everywhere — a gram of earth is likely to harbour 2,000,000 of them. Most bacteria live off either living or dead organic matter, but there are some able to survive in the primeval environments where nutrients are available only in the form of raw chemicals. Some grow and live solely on carbon dioxide from the air or water, and some on the energy released when sulphur, ammonia, hydrogen and iron are oxidized, for example. And almost certainly there are bacteria living in the primeval, 'lifeless' environment of the Kilimanjaro crater — especially in the warm, moist ground surrounding the fumaroles.

Created by recent geological activity and preserved by a hostile combination of altitude and climate, the Kilimanjaro crater today probably is a good example of the kind of environment which must have existed at the very beginnings of life on earth. And to pursue the analogy (though doubtless courting the dangers of over-simplification), you could view the 3,000 metre descent from summit to rain forest as a crude recapitulation of the evolution of terrestrial life from its beginning to the present day. As you scramble down the side of the mountain you seem to proceed from primitive to modern lifeforms, from a paucity of life to a profusion of it. In fact this impression is only valid in the broadest sense and, in any case, there is much more to evolution than those two very basic characteristics of change and numbers. But no matter, the analogy between the descent from the summit and the evolution of life on earth only arises because certain ecological laws fundamental to evolutionary development are also demonstrably at work on the slopes of Kilimanjaro, and the analogy is worth pursuing for that reason alone.

Ecology is about the interactions between living organisms and their environment; its basic tenet is that nothing can live for long in an environment to which it is not well-adapted. That is fairly obvious, you may say, as you stand panting at the summit of Kilimanjaro, enthralled by the view but nonetheless anxious to descend to more congenial climes where food tastes good and you sleep easily. But the tenet is not always obvious in quite the way that you might expect, which is precisely what makes the ecology of places like the upper slopes of Kilimanjaro so interesting.

Apart from the bacteria lurking about the crater — which are invisible anyway — the first form of life you encounter on the descent will be lichens. Those grey-green scruffy patches on the rocks. Now if the analogy between descent and evolution were to hold true, lichens ought to be the next most primitive organism after bacteria. And in one sense they are, though in fact they aren't. I will explain this apparent contradiction. The fossil record suggests that lichens are one or two hundred million years old while bacteria have existed for two or three thousand million years. After the bacteria many organisms arose before the advent of the lichens, the next most ancient being algae (the green threads and slime which accumulate in wet places) and fungi (mushrooms, toadstools and the like). Algae were the first organisms able to manufacture sugars by photosynthesis, so in effect were themselves the first food while fungi were the first organisms exclusively adapted to live off other organisms, either living or dead. Individually, algae and fungi have existed almost as long as bacteria, but since algae need a wet environment and fungi need some organic host, neither could survive in the dry sterile environment of places like the upper regions of Kilimanjaro. And neither did until relatively late in their careers, when some chance evolutionary development brought them together in the form of lichens.

Lichens are in fact *the* classic example of two independent organisms living together in symbiotic relationship — a mutually beneficial partnership which in the case of lichens enables both algae and fungus to live where neither could survive alone. On bare rock (and elsewhere) the fungus provides a comfortable environment in which the algae manufacture food for the partnership. And the benefits of the relationship not only extend the territorial range of the partners, in the case of the lichens which blotch the rocks of upper Kilimanjaro and elsewhere the benefits extend the lives of the partners as well. The rock lichens grow very slowly, perhaps as little as one millimetre in radius per year; some of the larger examples are hundreds of years old, and some in the Arctic are believed to be as much as 4,000 years old, which puts lichens among the oldest living things on earth. But while the algae and fungi achieve such remarkable longevity by living together in the form of a lichen, free-living individuals of their closest related species live for only a few months, or at most a few years, on their own. Why should they live longer in combination? No one knows for certain, but among conceivable explanations it has been suggested that lichens somehow are able to slow down the ageing process — an idea which inspired John Wyndham's science fiction novel *Trouble with Lichen*.

But whatever the explanation of their longevity, it is quite obvious that the lichens high on Kilimanjaro are perfectly adapted to their environment, though their sparseness is an indication of just how harsh an environment it is. But what do you make of the spiders which will be the next living thing encountered on the descent from the summit? The highest of them are found at about 5,000 metres. Small, dark-grey creatures darting in and out and over the loose shale. Well that is not particularly surprising, you might say, spiders are ubiquitous creatures which occur in the most unlikely places, so why not high on Kilimanjaro? But wait, spiders are carnivores, they eat other animals, mostly herbivores which in turn require some sort of vegetation to feed upon. Lichens are a form of vegetation, true enough, and probably they support a microscopic fauna, but the lichens themselves are very sparse above 5,000 metres and it is extremely unlikely that their total microbe population could be large enough to sustain all the spiders. So how do the spiders survive?

The precise explanation is not known. The spiders are probably salticids — jumping spiders — but in fact not even the species is known since no one has studied them, nor even collected them from that height on the mountain. Nonetheless, high altitude spiders have been studied elsewhere and, pending the definitive study of the Kilimanjaro population, it is not unreasonable to assume that their ecology and behaviour differs little from that of spiders living at high altitudes in other parts of the world. Such as those on Mount Everest, for example, which were first noted in 1924 and subsequently studied by the ecologist Dr L. W. Swan of the University of California in 1954 and again in 1960.

The Everest spiders are the highest inhabitants of the earth. The first specimens were found by a member of the British Expedition to Everest in 1924 among rocky debris at 6,500 metres, though there was no way of telling whether they resided permanently at that altitude or were vagrants blown in on the wind. This question of residential status aroused some controversy. As with the spiders on Kilimanjaro there seemed to be nothing for them to eat at 6,500 metres, though they seemed perfectly content there, and did not behave like vagrants swept unwillingly from a more congenial environment.

The controversy was finally resolved in 1961, when Dr Swan published the results of his investigations into the matter. The spiders were not blown in on the wind, Dr Swan reported, but instead were permanent residents provisioned by it. At altitudes up to 6,000 metres Dr Swan discovered many communities of spiders, small flies and other insects founded on windblown vegetation and fungi. It is a supremely simple food chain: the spiders eat the insects, the insects eat the vegetative debris, and the wind blows in enough to keep them all going. The spiders and insects survive the climatic extremes by spending most of their time several inches underground, it seems, where the temperature among the stones neither falls so low, nor climbs so high as at the surface. The insects are most active when the sun is up and, being less resistent to cold than the spiders, become torpid and easier to catch soon after it has gone — with the result that the spiders are most active in the sunless hours of the day. At night the whole community retreats — hibernates — before the cold. It is thought likely that the spiders enclose themselves in silken cells down among the rocky debris.

The spiders on the upper slopes of Kilimanjaro probably are also the last links of food chains provisioned by the wind, like those on the high Himalayas, but on the busy tourist route from Kibo Hut to Gillman's Point (where I saw most spiders), the windblown resources are supplemented with organic matter brought up on tourists' boots — not to mention the occasional discarded sandwich.

Spiders and lichens are increasingly common as you descend below 5,000 metres, and you may even see a raven or two rummaging for scraps around the Kibo Hut at 4,680 metres (unlike the all-black European raven, the African variety has a white collar), but you will not see any established flowering vegetation until you are on the Saddle and perhaps a good way below 4,500 metres.

The Saddle is a hostile environment: only three species of grass, one or two everlasting flowers and a couple of herbaceous plants are able to live there. And even they are very few and far between, each individual plant rooted deep in the shelter of some rock or hollow. The grasses usually seem more dead than alive, but they are likely to be the first thing you encounter on the descent which survives solely by converting the inorganic mountain into the organic building blocks of life, and insofar as this is true, the pioneer grasses represent the beginning of life on Kilimanjaro. A beginning from which life proliferates and diversifies as you descend through ever more congenial environments.

It has been said that because Kilimanjaro is so close to the equator, the high upper slopes experience 'summer every day and winter every night'. So that while journeying from Arctic to equator in just 2,000 metres the traveller on Kilimanjaro is also transported from summer to winter in a few hours. Both analogies sport the hazards of over-simplification but, nonetheless, they are a striking and essentially accurate description of the circumstances which have created the many remarkable environmental and floral features found on Kilimanjaro.

In terms of the life systems it supports, nothing quite like Kilimanjaro exists anywhere else in the world. But it is important to realize that the mountain's plant life is distinguished not so much by abundance and variety as by survival. Although the Kilimanjaro vegetation is exotic, it does not match the profusion and diversity you will find on other mountains in the region (the Usambaras, for example). Kilimanjaro does not invite you to admire a colourful display of unusual plants growing under optimum conditions so much as it offers a unique opportunity to observe plants adapted to survive in a series of unusually difficult environments. And the difficult environments are created by an unusual climate.

In general, the East African climate follows a very simple pattern of remarkable regularity. Two seasonal winds are responsible for it all. The south-east trade wind, moist from its passage over the Indian Ocean, brings the long rains which fall sometime between March and May; the north-east monsoon, relatively drier after a longer journey overland, brings the short rains which fall sometime between November and February. Dry periods follow the rains: a cold dry season at the middle of the year, a warm one at the end of it. That's the general pattern, but of course the local pattern varies considerably in its extent and timing, especially around Kilimanjaro, which constitutes such a massive obstruction to the winds as they blow in across the surrounding semi-arid plains. When the winds hit the mountain they are deflected upward; their moisture condenses as temperature and atmospheric pressure decrease, and then rain falls.

Most rain falls on the slopes between about a thousand and 3,000 metres, very little falls higher than that and hardly any reaches the lee side of the mountain. Thus the southern slopes of Kilimanjaro receive most of the longer and heavier rain carried by the south-east trade winds, while the northern slopes receive most of the shorter, lighter north-east monsoon. This marked difference in the amount of rain which falls on either side of the mountain produces an equally marked difference in the amount of vegetation which grows there. The northern slopes are more sparsely covered in general, and the forest belt, in particular, is much broader and denser on the southern slopes of the mountain than it is on the north.

And there is another factor which contributes to the more favourable climate prevailing on the southern side of the mountain. From May to October, while the south-east trade winds are already bringing the greater benefits of the long rains to the region, there is an 'anti-trade' wind blowing high above the system from the north-east. This is a dry wind, with a lower limit at between about 4,000 and 4,500 metres. As it crosses the Kilimanjaro massif, the anti-trade wind sweeps around the peaks, brushes the Saddle, and then, on the lee side of the mountain, combines with daily up-draught of warm air to create a counter-current which, in turn, concentrates the benefits of the moist south-east trade winds on the south-west slopes on the mountain, and sucks a significant amount of moisture high up the peak on that side. This meteorological phenomenon has made wheat farming a profitable exercise on south-west Kilimanjaro; it also provisions many of Kilimanjaro's high altitude spiders (remember the butterflies found on the upper slopes and glaciers), and, furthermore, it is responsible for a good proportion of the snow which lies on the peak.

Paradoxically, it seems that much of the snow crowning Kilimanjaro does not fall from clouds drifting above, but is the precipitation of clouds sucked up from below. If you were to spend any length of time on the Saddle around the middle of the year, you could not fail to notice that the early morning cloud cover frequently rises high above the south-west basin while remaining at a fairly constant level around the rest of the peak. At about 4,000 metres it reaches the dry anti-trade wind. If the anti-trade wind is blowing strongly — as is usual — the cloud is dissolved or driven away to the south, leaving the summit in unveiled sunshine while the slopes below are shaded. But occasionally the anti-trade wind is weaker, or is blowing at a higher altitude than usual; on such occasions cloud may rise to 6,000 metres or even more, huge banks of cumulus envelope the peak, and then snow falls.

Though the clouds only rarely rise high enough to deposit snow on the summit, they cover the south-west slopes almost every day in the season, so that the lower glaciers are protected from the sun during the hours when its melting effect would be greatest. This is why the glaciers have persisted longer and are most extensive on the south-west side of the mountain.

So, climatic circumstances bring more rain to the south side of Kilimanjaro than to the north, and the amount varies with altitude as the rain-bearing winds rise over the mountain. Rainfall also varies a great deal from year to year. You may imagine that the variables afflicting the mountain would deny it any sort of consistency, but in fact rainfall averages recorded at successive altitudes reveal a gradient which has produced a remarkably consistent pattern of vegetation all around the peak. The figures indicate that rainfall increases gradually as altitude decreases, from a minimum of perhaps less than 125 millimetres a year on the summit to a maximum of about 1,800 millimetres in the forest at 2,000 metres (below the forest rainfall decreases again to about 500 millimetres a year on the plains at 750 metres). The gradual increase in rainfall down the slopes of the mountain matches the progression from a paucity to a profusion of life which was noted earlier in this chapter. And of course that is no coincidence. Water is life's solvent, nothing survives without it, and where there is more water there is always more life. But on Kilimanjaro the increase in rainfall at descending altitudes is overlaid with other significant environmental factors. Extremes of temperature, for example, the temperature range and the intensity of solar radiation, also vary with altitude. The result is that the Kilimanjaro vegetation does not simply increase in quantity with the increasing rainfall down the slopes, it falls into a remarkable sequence of distinct vegetation zones as well, each zone characterized by the types of plant best adapted to survive under that particular set of environmental conditions. The zones girdle the mountain, one above the other. Their altitude, breadth and density on any particular slope is governed by local conditions of rainfall, temperature and so forth, but their characteristics remain consistent right around the mountain — though frequently demonstrating survival close to the limits of existence more than profusion under optimum conditions.

There are five zones, easily recognized by their vegetation, but best defined first of all in terms of average rainfall and altitude. Following the tourist route down the south-eastern slopes of the mountain the first zone is — naturally enough — the *summit zone,* which extends from the top down to about 5,000 metres and probably receives less than 125 millimetres of rain a year on average. Second is the *alpine zone,* extending down to about 4,200 metres and including the Saddle where rainfall is about 250 millimetres a year. Third is the *moorland zone,* which goes down to about 3,600 metres and includes the Horombo region where rainfall averages 635 millimetres a year. Fourth is the *heather zone,* extending down to 2,700 metres at Mandara, for example, where rainfall has averaged 1,676 millimetres a year. Fifth is the *montane forest zone,* wherein the rainfall average is 1,800 millimetres per year at 2,000 metres. At one time there was a *lowland forest* below the montane forest, but it has been replaced by agriculture and settlement.

And what are the distinctive features of the zones? Well, the summit zone has the lichens and the spiders already mentioned which, though interesting, need not detain you for long. The alpine zone is another matter. You could cross it in a couple of hours if you wished, but it deserves rather more attention than such a swift crossing could afford. Few other places on earth provide such a good opportunity to observe life at the limits of its existence.

The upper parts of the zone, and the Saddle in particular, have been called an alpine desert and surely deserve the title. You can see by the colour of the landscape that nothing much has ever grown there. The earth is brown, yellow and grey, rusted, loose and sandy — a sterile expanse of finely ground rock, doubtless well endowed with the chemicals from which plants are built, but almost totally lacking both the organic matter which makes a good soil and the climatic conditions which promote plant growth. Rainfall averages less than 250 millimetres per year on the Saddle and, since most of it quickly drains away through the porous earth, plants can survive only where moisture is trapped by some feature of the terrain. Hence the sparse nature of the vegetation in the upper parts of the zone. Lower down, where more rain falls, there is more vegetation. But, while rainfall certainly determines the amount of vegetation growing in any given part of the zone, drought resistance is not the only determinant of its overall character. There are other factors at work too — principally stemming from a harsh daily round of frost and scorching sunshine.

Ground temperatures throughout the alpine zone may reach forty degrees centigrade any day of the year when the sun is shining, for example, and may stand below freezing for nine or ten hours every night. So 'summer every day and winter every night' is not just a catchy phrase — it really is an accurate description of climatic conditions in the alpine zone. And while many plants around the world are able to live through either long hot summers or hard winters, very few indeed can survive where the extremes of summer and winter both occur in the course of just one day — every day. And those few survive only by virtue of their special adaptations. But let's begin with the problems.

In the morning the problem confronting plants in the alpine zone is not so much the temperature extremes as the rapid transition from one extreme to another. The thin air at those high altitudes absorbs very little heat, so that with the sky clear most mornings leaves begin to warm up almost as soon as the sun strikes them — certainly well before the ground is fully thawed. Plants deal with heat by exhaling water vapour from their leaves and other surfaces (transpiration — an essential

Characteristic plants on Kilimanjaro at *above:* 4,500m in the alpine vegetation zone

Below: 3,600m in the moorland zone

Right: 2,700m in the heather zone

Top: mosses and lichens grow up to an altitude of 5,300m on Kilimanjaro

Right: grasses occur up to about 4,700m wherever pockets of moisture persist, as here beside rocks on the western shoulder

Above: Arabis alpina, identical to the familiar bedding plant, is found up to nearly 5,000m on the mountain

The giant groundsels (*left*) and lobelias (*above*) are relatives of the common plants uniquely adapted to equatorial high altitudes. The leaf rosette closes to protect the delicate growing bud from night frosts

Next page: giant groundsels in the moorland zone at 3,700m, above Horombo

Giant heather, lichens, grasses and flowers of the heather zone, above Mandara at 2,700m

Next page left: giant heather swathed in lichen at 2,700m

Right: forest trees draped with mosses at 2,400m

Views in the montane forest zone on the southern slopes of Kilimanjaro

Next page: a panoramic view in the Kilimanjaro forest, climax of the mountain's vegetation

The delicate *Impatiens kilimanjari* is common in the Kilimanjaro forest, but is not known in any other part of the world

life process of plants). Transpiration, of course, depends upon the flow of water to the leaves from the roots and ultimately from the soil. But water flow within a plant is severely impeded if the soil and roots are frozen or even very cold. When water flow is impeded transpiration soon drains the plant, which then wilts and dies.

So the first problem of the day confronting plants in the alpine zone is simply to survive the critical period when the sun is so hot while the ground is still frozen. The second problem is to complete the essential functions (photosynthesis, growth, reproduction and so forth) during the rest of the day while the sunshine remains potentially excessive and the frost moderates but slightly.

Solar radiation is the major part of the problem. With Kilimanjaro so close to the equator, and the air around its upper slopes so thin and clean, the solar radiation which strikes the alpine zone on a clear day is extraordinarily intense, with a much higher proportion of ultraviolet rays than reaches lower and temperate regions. The sunburn which quickly afflicts unprotected human skin will attest to the ferocity of the Kilimanjaro sunshine, and its effects are no less harmful to unprotected plant tissue. Increased transpiration is a plant's customary response to increased sunshine, but such a response would not suffice in the alpine zone any more than increased sweating would protect exposed human skin. In the first instance the beneficial effects of transpiration are quickly dissipated by the rapid evaporation of moisture into the dry thin air, and secondly, water supply is limited and not always flowing freely, as we have seen. So plants need something more effective than transpiration to protect them from the intense solar radiation which falls on the alpine zone. And having survived the sun by day, they must then be prepared for the frost by night — the third major problem which affects the character of the alpine zone vegetation.

The temperature of sunlit surfaces in the zone may reach extremely high levels, but the thin air surrounding them is never very warm. A rock surface at noon may register forty degrees centigrade while the air temperature stands at eight degrees. And when the sun is obscured all surfaces quickly lose heat to the cool air; even a passing cloud may cause a ten degree drop and at sunset the temperature falls very rapidly indeed. On a clear evening the ground will actually be colder than the air within an hour or two of sunset. Surface water freezes while the air a metre above is still one or two degrees above zero. This temperature inversion is caused by longwave radiation from the ground to the sky; a strong local wind may develop in the valleys as the denser cold air at ground level drains away down the mountain beneath the relatively warmer air which had accumulated above during the day.

Anyone camped out in the alpine zone soon experiences the surprising severity of the nightly frosts, and soon learns that comfort demands more insulation beneath the sleeping bag than above it. The plants established there also must be adapted in some way to withstand the regular freezing conditions, but apart from the obvious need to protect their delicate young shoots and flowers (which would die if frozen), plants must also contend with the threat of being quite literally heaved out of the ground by a curious phenomenon which occurs under such conditions called solifluction.

Solifluction is caused by the daily alternate freezing and thawing of any moisture present in the top few centimetres of the soil. The moisture freezes into bundles of ice needles which stand vertically in the soil, rising some slight distance above the surface. The needles are frequently capped with stones and soil particles, and below ground their formation vigorously disturbs the soil. When the needles melt the next morning the moisture gathers most readily where the soil is most disturbed; more needles are formed there again the following night, more disturbance occurs . . . and so on.

This cycle of freezing and thawing has a sorting effect on the soil, stones and larger particles tend to be graded and gathered together by size and eventually a pattern emerges. In coarse-textured soil on flat ground you will find distinct polygons marked out by cracks and rimmed with stones. On sloping ground you will see parallel stone stripes — those places on the Saddle where the stones seem to have been raked into lines are a typical example.

By its very nature, solifluction only occurs on moist bare ground, where its occurrence inevitably constitutes a formidable hindrance to the establishment of the vegetative cover that would inhibit it. In fact only moss is capable of residing permanently on an active solifluction surface without the benefits of some modifying agent. Moss succeeds by adopting a free-rolling lifestyle, literally riding the daily round of frost and thaw without any fixed attachment to the soil. You will find balls, discs and sausages of moss lying completely loose on many active solifluction surfaces around Kilimanjaro, especially along the route under the southern glaciers. The moss grows around a core of soil or other matter (leopard or other animal droppings in some cases, I suspect) and thereafter is unaffected by the restless soil beneath. The mosses rise on the ice needles at night and fall as they melt the next day. The motion turns the mosses constantly, enabling many to grow equally on all sides, so that they eventually form perfect spheres and cylinders.

Solifluction, solar radiation, temperature variation, drought. These, then, are the major problems that plants must overcome to become established in the alpine zone on Kilimanjaro. The problems are most severe at the top, so it may seem surprising that the first vegetation encountered on the descent is nothing other than a few tufts of grass. No remarkable adaptations to an exceptionally harsh environment demonstrated here, you might say. After all, grass is the most conspicuous vegetation found anywhere on earth. And that, in fact, is precisely the point. It would be surprising if grass was *not* among the highest vegetation on Kilimanjaro. Grass is the archetypal pioneer plant: one or another of its many forms is usually the first plant to become established wherever the earth lies bare. So the adaptation manifested by the scruffy tufts which represent the beginnings of life on Kilimanjaro lies not so much in the individual species as in the capacity of grass generally to increase, colonize and persist.

The grass species high on Kilimanjaro share the characteristics of all grasses that manifest an opportunistic lifestyle. They have extensive root systems, mature quickly and produce an abundance of seed. Thin leaves minimize the effects of excessive solar radiation, and microscopic roothairs trap the minute droplets of water which condense underground as the temperature falls even in relatively dry weather. Furthermore, the high Kilimanjaro grasses grow in the form of a tussock and this is crucial to survival in their particular environment. The tussock is a dense, felt-like mass of dead or dying stalks and leaves. It may be fifty millimetres or more thick and may spread over a considerable area. Its function is to protect tender young shoots from dangerous extremes of temperature. In a typical instance, a botanist found that while the temperature of the surrounding air stood at minus five degrees centigrade, it was plus two point five degrees at the heart of the tussock and plus three degrees among the roots immediately beneath. Such effective insulation both protects emergent shoots during the vulnerable first stages of growth and maximizes waterflow within the plant during its remarkably brief maturation period. And in addition to the benefits of temperature insulation, the tussock serves to buffer moisture variations too: like a tight, well-insulated wad of felt the tussock holds rain or mist water for a long time.

The insulation effect of tussock grasses will also stabilize surfaces susceptible to solifluction if they manage to become established during a relatively mild period when solifluction does not occur. So too will several herbs (*Subularia monticola,* for example), and plants with deep tap-roots (*Haplosciadium abyssinicum*) which are able to thrust their roots well beneath the solifluction surface. As with the tussock grasses, these plants form a blanket, or cushion, over the soil which creates a small stable area of more amenable temperature. Solifluction no longer occurs, the area becomes suitable for slightly less hardy vegetation, and a community of plants is created that will undoubtedly provide accommodation for a number of invertebrate animals. Spiders, weevils, earwigs and other insects which, given the chance, can readily adapt themselves to the overriding demands of extremely harsh environments.

The insects' adaptations may be of an unexpected nature. The entomologist George Salt found, for example, that the entire insect population of the Kilimanjaro alpine zone was either sedentary or distinctly unwilling to fly. Salt assumed this was probably because every flying insect was likely to be blown far from the essential benefits of its limited home habitat by the prevailing stiff breezes, which would constitute a strong selection pressure in favour of staying in one place. In the alpine desert, where conditions are especially severe, Salt found that the insect population was not only unwilling, but also largely unable to fly. Representatives of species which sport wings in more congenial environments lack them entirely in the alpine desert. This probably results from their adoption of a cryptozoic habit — that is, a hidden lifestyle. When not actually concealed among the available vegetation, the insects high on Kilimanjaro (like those on the Himalayas mentioned earlier in this chapter), escape the excesses of radiation and temperature by living underground. The insects' adoption of a cryptozoic habit is their principal adaptation to the rigours of the upper Kilimanjaro environments, says Salt, and of course it renders wings superfluous.

Now back to plants. Of the four major problems confronting plants in the alpine zone, solifluction is relatively localized, affecting only the plants which find themselves attempting to grow where it occurs. But the other three problems — solar radiation, temperature variation and drought — affect the zone as a whole, as we have seen, and to counter their adverse effects plants must adopt more general adaptations. Insulation is the crux of the matter: insulation to limit the demands of transpiration on an already precarious water supply; insulation against the dangers of excessive radiation and insulation to buffer the violent extremes of temperature.

The various (and quite numerous) adaptations which fulfil the function of insulating the alpine zone vegetation against the dangers of its environment are not difficult to identify. In general, they constitute the most striking feature of any particular plant, or plant community. The silver sheen which washes over the landscape as the wind rustles through the vegetation of the lower zone indicates, for example, that very many plants have shiny, light-coloured surfaces which reflect most of the incident solar radiation. On closer inspection you will find that many plants are densely covered with fine white hairs; leaves are often quite small in relation to the size of the plant, they might be hairy, or have a thick leathery skin. These are all general attributes which serve to control transpiration and provide insulation against temperature extremes in various species.

At the same time, some plants have features specific to their particular form and circumstance. Stiff white blossoms, for example, help the everlasting flowers (*Helichrysum sp.*) to thrive in the high exposed areas where no other flower can. And plants with thin woody stems which are liable to freeze overnight, have leaves particularly adapted to delay transpiration while the stems thaw next morning. *Alchemilla* (a common shrub of the lower zone), for example, has small hairy leaves which are crinkled to further reduce the amount of sunshine falling on the plant's transpiration surfaces. For the same reason *Euryops dacrydioides* (another shrub of the lower zone, distinguished by its clusters of bright yellow flowers) has leaves so small that they amount to little more than minute green scales packed tightly around the stem.

The rosette plants, on the other hand, grow so close to the ground that their stems are virtually non-existent. Their dense wad of leaves insulates the ground beneath from extreme cold, so there is little chance of frost impeding waterflow through the plant and, with the leaves so close to the roots, little distance for the water to travel. Consequently, the rosette plants (*Haplocarpha rueppellii, Conyza subscaposa, Oreophyton falcatum, Nannoseris schimperi,* for example), can maintain relatively large, fleshy, thin leaves with few of the drought-resistant and transpiration controls which are usually the most conspicuous features of the plants which grow higher above ground.

The adaptations which aid the survival of plants in the alpine zone tend to be most obvious at the higher altitudes, where conditions are most extreme, but of course they are present in representatives of the same species throughout the zone, and lower down, where rainfall is more propitious, the plants and their adaptations are more luxuriantly displayed. As you descend through the alpine zone it will be clear that luxuriance increases with increasing rainfall down the slopes of the mountain. The mean scruffy tussocks of the first grasses, the straggly everlasting flowers of the Saddle, the flattened rosettes and spindly shrubs of the upper zone — all plants become larger, grander and more distinctive with decreasing altitude. *Alchemilla* is much more common, thickets of *Euryops* occur, dense banks of everlasting flowers, and tussocks like footstools with a head of fine green grass. Clumps of heath appear along the track, and suddenly you realise that the landscape has assumed the aspect of a moorland.

The boundary between the alpine and moorland zones lies at different altitudes on the various slopes of the mountain, but wherever adequate water is available it is best marked by plants manifesting the most distinctive and striking features that any on the mountain have adopted to counter the problems of their environments. These are giant groundsels and lobelias. Weird plants made familiar by their names but in reality quite unlike anything which exists anywhere but in such high equatorial environments.

The giant groundsels (*Senecio sp.*) and the giant lobelias (*Lobelia sp.*) belong to the same genera, respectively, as the weed and the delicate bedding plant which are familiar to gardeners everywhere. This means that botanists consider the two groundsels and the two lobelias to be as closely related as, for instance, the great tit and the blue tit, or the brown and the rainbow trout. Botanical classification of this kind is based principally upon the structure of the reproductive organs — the flowers — and in this respect the relationship of the Kilimanjaro giants to their common garden counterparts is indisputable. Everything else — their size, their growth pattern, their lifestyle, even their behaviour, is directly related to the problems of living high on Kilimanjaro. The weird and peculiar features of the giant groundsels and lobelias may seem to belie their botanical classification, but those features are, in fact, simply the adaptations that have arisen within two very common genera to meet the demands of a very uncommon environment.

The plants themselves are unmistakable. The groundsels generally stand up to about four metres high, with a distinctly top-heavy, off-balance look which undoubtedly adds to their air of improbability. The stem is thick and covered with a dense, felt-like mass of dead leaves. Two or three branches may be present (looking more like ill-considered appendages than genuine limbs), each as thick as the stem and each crowned with a luxuriant cabbage of leaves up to one metre wide from which the flowering stem emerges in season. The distribution of the groundsels within their zone is determined by the availability of water (they need a good and reliable supply and their presence in a particular valley or ranged along the foot of a cliff is in itself an indication that water is locally abundant), and their form is determined by the need to maintain a substantial waterflow from the roots to the large leaves. As might be expected, insulation is once again the crux of the matter. But not insulation to restrict water demand, as with the plants in the upper reaches of the alpine zone, but rather insulation to ensure a constant and adequate supply of water to the large leaves which in turn are needed to insulate the large but delicate growing shoot of the plant. The outer leaves of the groundsel rosette may be over half a metre long and 200 to 230 millimetres broad, but they possess hardly any of the drought-resistant, insulation features which are such a conspicuous feature of the high alpine zone vegetation. Groundsel leaves are shiny enough to reflect some incident radiation, and have a slight covering of hair, but in general their form invites rather than restricts transpiration. So does their behaviour.

At night the groundsel's rosette of leaves closes tightly around the delicate central bud, maintaining an interior temperature several degrees centigrade above zero while the surrounding air temperature may fall several degrees below. By morning the entire plant may be rimed with frost, but the rosette opens to the sun as soon as it rises, principally because such a large plant must get on with the business of growing early in the day. However, an early start means that transpiration will begin to place heavy demands upon the plant's waterflow system long before the temperature of its environment has risen above zero. The groundsel manifests two adaptations which deal with this crucial problem. The first, perhaps not surprisingly, is the dense blanket of dead leaves around the stem which ensures that the water transport system inside can never freeze. The blanket consists solely of the leaves which droop and die at the base of the rosette as the emergent bud grows upward. The groundsels grow very slowly (it has been estimated that specimens two metres high could be a hundred years old), so the blanket steadily builds up and consolidates as the dying leaves contract around the lengthening stem. Eventually it becomes a dense dry mass of almost mummified leaf remains, several centimetres thick, maintaining above zero temperatures within the stem while the air outside is below freezing.

But of course an unfrozen stem is of little use in the early morning, while the ground itself may be frozen and prevailing low temperatures impede the absorption of water from the soil and through the roots. Water flow may be possible, but water uptake is severely restricted, so the groundsels have a second adaptation to ensure adequate supply to their transpiration surfaces during the critical hours: water storage reservoirs. Their pith and cortex (the hard layer immediately beneath the insulating blanket) are constructed of thin-walled, open cells which render the plant strong but light (as you will find if you lift a dead specimen), and clearly capable of holding enough water to maintain the plant's water balance when demand is high and supply impeded.

Water supply is also crucial to the giant lobelias on Kilimanjaro. Like the groundsels they need a substantial amount and grow only where it is available; they also grow in the form of a rosette, but they are not so large, nor does their rosette of leaves stand from a stem any distance above the ground. The leaves are smaller, thinner, and more regularly organized than in the case of the groundsel; giving the lobelia more the appearance of an artichoke than of a cabbage.

Each night the leaves of the lobelias close tightly around the central bud, and each morning they unfold to the rising sun, as with the groundsels, but without quite the same water balance problems that confront the larger giants. To begin with, transpiration from the smaller leaf surfaces of the lobelias is, of course, less demanding, secondly the plant grows closer to the ground and therefore its water supply does not have to travel so far, and thirdly, being so close to the ground and itself well insulated, the lobelias probably moderate the temperatures which would otherwise occur in the soil around their roots.

The insulation strategy of the lobelias consists essentially of the ability of their leaves to close and enfold the central core of the plant, but it is aided by watery fluid which the plant holds at the base of each leaf. The quantity of fluid stored in this way will be amply demonstrated by the soaked trouser leg of anyone who knocks against a lobelia rosette, but it is not supplied by rain alone, for the reservoirs will be full even after a long dry spell.

Obviously the plant secretes some fluid of its own, and it has been suggested that it is a form of anti-freeze. Could be; certainly a denser and more viscous fluid than water will be found beneath the small crescents of ice which lie in the reservoirs after a frosty night, and any such fluid could only enhance the insulation of the inner plant.

The delicate blue flowers by which the giant lobelias are classified are neatly arranged, in their hundreds, spiralling up and around the stout pillar which eventually emerges from the rosette. The pillar may be a metre and a half high and over 300 millimetres thick, it grows quickly, insulated along its length by the dense bracts which protect by night and open by day to expose the tiny flowers. The individual flowers are no larger than those found on the common garden lobelia — an incidental observation that may help to persuade the sceptic that, as with the groundsels and so much else of the alpine zone vegetation, it really is the demands of local conditions and not the plants' generic origins which are responsible for the size and shape of the lobelias on Kilimanjaro. Further persuasion may be found in the fact that almost identical plants have evolved in similar environments on the Andes near the equator in Peru. But not from representatives of the *Lobelia* and *Senecio* genera; no, the South American examples have evolved in the *Espeletia,* a quite different genus whose species include the cultivated Lion's Ear. Together, these plants from the Andes and East Africa present a striking example of parallel evolution: that is, similar adaptations have evolved in different plants from distant, but very similar environments.

Kilimanjaro's giant lobelias and groundsels are among just fifty-five species which Olov Hedberg, author of the definitive work on the flora of the high East African mountains, lists from above 4,000 metres on the mountain. That there are so few is eloquent demonstration of what has been termed the 'floral poverty' of Kilimanjaro. Fifty-five species may indeed constitute poverty of the numerical kind, but the survival of even that number under such demanding conditions raises of wealth of intriguing questions: Kilimanjaro is relatively young, its alpine slopes must have been bare of vegetation until comparatively recently; so where did the plants come from? How did they get there? Why have fifty-five species been able to adapt to the environment while others have not? By what processes or mechanisms did the essential adaptations arise?

These rather simple and basic questions were among the first that scientists asked concerning the vegetation of Kilimanjaro. Several hypotheses were available in those early days, and it was hoped that investigations on the mountain would either support or confound them, but such has not been the case. A great deal of information has indeed been collected, which may lend support to one hypothesis rather than another, but indisputable answers to the questions remain elusive.

However, it is known that about forty per cent of the plants found in the alpine zone do not occur elsewhere in the immediate surroundings of the mountain. Of these, some are endemic (that is, they occur only on Kilimanjaro), some are found on other high mountains in East Africa, some occur in South Africa only, some in the Himalayas, some in Europe and some are found all around the world. One plant, *Arabis alpina,* which flourishes in sheltered niches high on the mountain is identical to the cultivated garden plant of the same name which is common throughout the world. Olov Hedberg has even cross-pollinated specimens of *Arabis alpina* from East Africa with others from Lapland and raised second and third generations from the resultant seed which matched the form of the parent plants. Why is *Arabis alpina* so widespread? Migration, or dispersal are the only possible explanations. Either the plants progressively migrated, in short stages, from one congenial environment to the next as climatic changes varied environmental conditions; or its seeds were dispersed greater distances by the wind, by cyclones perhaps, or on the feet of birds. But why was *Arabis* able to survive, unchanged, in such a variety of environments? We do not know; we can only say that, like the grasses, *Arabis* must be adaptively predisposed to a pioneer lifestyle.

And in contrast to *Arabis* there are the plants which are endemic to Kilimanjaro. The groundsels and the lobelias, for example, are the result of very considerable adaptations. Of course, we know that climate and environment were the fundamental cause, but why did they need to adapt? and how were the adaptations achieved? Again, we do not know. It has been suggested that excessive radiant heat could have produced mutations in seed exposed to a volcanic eruption, perhaps giving the plant some advantageous adaptation which then became genetically fixed in the species and was passed to future generations. A series of eruptions could have produced a series of mutations, ultimately producing the well-adapted plants we see today. It is only an hypothesis, but it could have happened.

In respect of groundsel and lobelia evolution it has also been suggested that the plants show a progressive evolutionary trend up the mountain. There are species of each found at discreet levels from the forest upward, and the distinctions between them could be said to lie in the direction of adaptation to increasingly severe environmental conditions. The hypothesis here is that, starting from the basic forest stock, mutant plants with some advantageous adaptation became established in niches progressively higher up the mountain. The adaptations became fixed, different species arose at different levels. Again it could have happened — the staggering capacity of vegetation in general to seize every opportunity and maximize every advantage hardly needs to be emphasized. In fact, as you pass from the alpine zone, through the moorland zone to the heather zone and the forest, through a gradual progression from paucity to profusion, you may conclude that it is more imagination, rather than more observation, which is needed to answer the simple and basic questions of the Kilimanjaro vegetation.

In the moorland zone, the prevailing rainfall, radiation and temperature conditions which so restricted the growth of vegetation higher up the mountain have become positively beneficial. Rainfall is reasonable though not abundant, sunshine is less damaging, frost is neither so frequent nor so severe. Life is easier, and as a result the vegetation steadily becomes more extensive, more dense and more luxuriant at descending altitudes. The grasses are still of a tussock form, but of different species: denser, much grander tussocks than above. Anemones and violets are found under sheltered banks. There are more birds and more evidence of animal life — altogether, the environment becomes more gentle.

The heaths which dominate the heather zone continue the trend. While dense but spindly thickets of *Philippia jaegeri* may be plentiful at 3,500 metres, there is a heather 'woodland' of *Erica arborea* at 2,700 metres. Instead of man-high shrubs these are trees, six metres high with trunks up to half a metre thick. From a grassland of knee-high tussocks, dotted with ericas, herbs and lilies, you walk into a grove of heather. Gnarled like old olive trees, their branches draped with skeins of lichen. There are shrubs and flowers, bracken and even a form of blackberry. The environment begins to seem like a place where men could live and then, quite suddenly, the heather woodland is replaced by even larger trees, and you enter the forest.

Forests are climax vegetation, they will eventually appear wherever there is enough water and the right amount of sunshine. The montane forest on the lower slopes of Kilimanjaro is the climax of all the trends that the journey down the mountain has followed. It receives the highest rainfall, enjoys the most beneficial combination of sunshine and temperature extremes, contains the grandest vegetation and sustains the greatest biomass. It is also a welcoming place.

Each time I entered the Kilimanjaro forest after a spell on the upper slopes I was struck by a wonderful sense of relief. It was like a homecoming — there was shelter, water, and even food if I searched for it. They say that mankind evolved from a forest environment, so perhaps my relief sprang from a sense of continuity evoked by the resilience and quiet splendour of the trees around me.

There is a timeless quality to every virgin tropical forest; they all may be havens for the traveller too, but the Kilimanjaro forest has a unique third quality: it is a buffer between two powerful and incompatible trends. Above, 3,000 square kilometres of mountain hold an unparalleled example of life's progression from barren arctic shale to lush forest. Below, man's exploitation advances — a progression of endeavour extending from the marginal rangelands where nomads herd their stock, through towns and cities, wheat and coffee farms, to the smallholdings where people like Samja and Francis plant their maize on the mountain slopes. The contrast between these two trends is enormous, and their implications merit contemplation as you pass from one to the other through the surviving narrow belt of unmolested forest that girdles Kilimanjaro.

Acknowledgements

Many people contributed to the preparation of this book: the men who guided me around the mountain; the kindly folk who accommodated me before and after the climbs; the scientists and librarians who assisted my research; the publishers and printers who brought words and pictures together. I am deeply grateful to them all.

The photograph of the leopard corpse in the second section of photographs is reproduced by courtesy of Mme E. von Lany.

Bibliography and further reading

Ballard F. M. 1962
Volcanoes in History, Theory and Eruption

Barth G. 1863
Letter on Kilimanjaro
Atheneum 1866: 149

Beke C. T. 1849
The Discovery of Kilimanjaro
Atheneum 1119:357; 1124:488

Bigger M.
A Checklist of the Flora of Kilimanjaro
Reprint (with additions) from Ice Cap 4

Bridges R. C. 1976
*W. D. Cooley, the Royal Geographical Society and
African geography in the 19th Cent.*

Brodie F. M. 1967
The Devil Drives, Life of Burton.

Bruce E. A. 1934
The Giant Lobelias of East Africa

Burton R. F. 1858
Progress of expedition to East Africa
J.Roy.Geog.Soc. 28:188—

—1858
East Africa Coast Expedition
Blackwoods Magazine

—1858-59
Reports and comment on East Africa Expedition
Proc.Roy.Geog.Soc. 3: 115, 116, 208, 211, 213, 304,
306.

—1859
Report on East Africa Expedition
J.Roy.Geog.Soc. 29: 1-464

—1864
On Cooley and Kilimanjaro
Atheneum 1899:407

Coe M. J. 1967
Ecology of Mount Kenya
Monog.Biol. 17

—1979
*Micro climate and animal life in the equatorial
mountains*
Zool.Afr.4(2): 101-128

Collinson A. S. 1977
Introduction to World Vegetation

Cooley W. D. 1845
The Geography of N'yassi
Proc.Roy.Geog.Soc. 15:185

—1849
The discovery of Kilimanjaro
Atheneum 1125:516

—1852
Inner Africa Laid Open

—1863
Kilimanjaro and von der Decken
Atheneum: 178; 226; 332; 609.

—1864
Kilimanjaro and the RGS
Atheneum:84

Cotton A. D. 1930
A visit to Kilimanjaro
Kew Bull. 3:97-121

Coupland R. 1938
East Africa and its Invaders

—1939
Exploitation of East Africa 1856-90

Decken C. C. von der 1886
On the Snowy Mountains of East Equatorial Africa
Proc.Roy.Geog.Soc. 8:5

Downie C. 1964
Glaciations of Mount Kilimanjaro
Geol.Soc.Am.Bull. 75:1-26

Downie C. Humphries D. W., Wilcockson W. H.,
Wilkinson P. 1956
Geology of Kilimanjaro
Nature 178:828-830

Downie C., Wilkinson P. 1972
The Geology of Kilimanjaro

Dundas C. 1924
Kilimanjaro and its People

Fosbrooke H. A. 1962
Richard Thornton in East Africa
Tanzania Notes and Records 58:43-63

Gaskell T. F., Morris M. 1979
World Climate, the weather, the environment and man

Geilinger W. 1936
The Retreat of the Kilimanjaro Glaciers
Tanzania Notes & Records 2:7-20

Gillman C. 1923
An Ascent of Kilimanjaro
Geog.J.61: 1-27

Hatchell G. W. 1956
*Queen Victoria, Kilimanjaro and the Kenya/Tanganyika
boundary*
Tanzania notes and Records 43:41

Hamilton W. J. 1849
Royal Geographical Society Presidential Address
Proc.Roy.Geog.Soc. 19: ix-xvi

Hedberg O. 1948
Vegetation Belts on East African mountains
Svensk.Bot.Tid. 45

—1955
Altitudinal Zonation of the vegetation on the East African mountains
Proc.Linn.Soc.Lond. 165(1952-53)2: June 55 134-136

—1961
The Phytogeographical position of the Afroalpine Flora
Univ. Toronto Press

—1962
Intercontinental Crosses in Arabis alpina
Carylogia 15:253-260

—1964
Features of Afroalpine Plant Ecology
Acta Phytogeographica Suecica 49

—1965
Afroalpine flora elements
Webbia 19(2):519-529

—1969
Evolution and speciation in a tropical high mountain flora
Biol.J.Linn.Soc 1:135-148

—1969
Growth rates of the EA Giant Senecios
Nature 222:163-4

—1970
Evolution of the Afroalpine Flora
Biotropica 2(1):16-23

—1979
Tropical alpine life-forms of vascular plants
Oikos 33:297-307

Höehnel L. V. 1894
Discovery by Count Teleki of Lakes Rudolf and Stefanie

Hohn A. 1962
The spider fauna of the East African mountains.
Zool.Bidrag.Fran.Uppsala 35

Hollis C. 1958
Note on von der Decken
Tanzania Notes and Records 50:63-67

Hooker J. D. 1873
On the subalpine vegetation of Kilimanjaro
J.Linn.Soc. 14:141-146

Huxley J. 1942
Kilimanjaro volcanic activity
Letter to the Times 30 Dec 1942

Illustrated London News 1943
Active or Extinct? The problem of Kilimanjaro
202:80-81

Ingrams W. H. 1931
Zanzibar, its history and people.

Johnston H. H. 1885
The Kilimanjaro expedition
Proc.Roy.Geog.Soc.7(3) conf. 137

Journal of Glaciology 1951—
Reports on the early history of glaciology
1:142-44; 294; 388-391; 510; 576-77. 4: 124-7; 371-72; 819-20.

Krapf L. 1843—
Journal and letters in Church Missionary Society Archives

—1860
Travels, Researches and Missionary Labours in East Africa

Kent P. E. 1944
Kilimanjaro: An Active Volcano
Nature 153:454-5

Kersten O. 1871
Decken's Reisen in Ost Afrika

Lamb H. H. 1977
Climate, Present, Past and Future vol. 2

Livingstone D. 1856
On 'snowy' mountains in Africa
Proc.Roy.Geog.Soc 1:243

Mabberley D. J. 1974
The pachycaul Lobelias of Africa and St. Helena
Kew Bulletin 29(3):535-584

Mathew G. 1975
The Periplus of the Erythrean Sea
in: Chittick N. & Rotberg R. L. 1975
East Africa and The Orient

Meyer H. 1890
Across East African Glaciers

—1891
Zur Kenntnis von Eis und Schnee des Kilimandscharo
Wissenschaftl. Veröffentl. d. Ver.f.Erdk.zu Lpzg 1

—1899
Gletscher des Kilimandscharo
Geographische Zeitschrift 5: heft 4.

—1900
Der Kilimandjaro

Moreau R. E. 1933
Pleistocene Climatic Changes and the Distribution of life in East Africa
J.Ecology 21:415-435

—1936
A contribution to the ornithology of Kilimanjaro and Meru
Proc.Zool.Soc.Lond. 1935:843-891

Murchison R. I. 1856
Livingstone, and comment on Kilimanjaro discovery
Proc.Roy.Geog.Soc 1:243-4

—1857
On Kilimanjaro and Burton expedition
Proc.Roy.Geog.Soc 1:450

—1863
On von der Decken expedition to Kilimanjaro
Proc.Roy.Geog.Soc. 8:2

Needham J. and Lu Gwei-Djen 1961
The earliest Snow Crystal Observations
Weather 16(1961)10:319-327

New C. 1872
Letter to Dr Kirk
Proc.Roy.Geog.Soc 16:161

—1872
Account of Kilimanjaro ascent
Alpine J. 6:51

—1874
Life, Wanderings and Labours in East Africa

Oliver D. and Hooker J. D. 1885
Plants collected by Thomson J. in East Africa
J.Linn.Soc.21:392-406

Oliver R. 1957
Sir Harry Johnston and the Scramble for Africa

Petermann A. 1862
Letters on Kilimanjaro
Atheneum 1862: 194; 298

Polemin N. 1960
Introduction to Plant Geography

Rebmann J. 1845
Journal and letters in Church Missionary Society Archives

—1849
Journey to Jagga, the snow country of East Africa
Church Missionary Intelligencer 1

— and Erhardt 1856
Map of the East African Interior
Proc.Roy.Geog.Soc.1.

Reusch R. 1928
Report of Kilimanjaro ascents
Tanganyika Times 10 Feb 1928

Richard J. J. 1945
Volcanic observations in East Africa
J. East African Nat.Hist.Soc 18: 1-12

—1945
Kilimanjaro crater fumaroles and seismic activity during 1942-45
Nature 156:352-4

Richards P. W. 1952
The Tropical Rainforest

Richardson D. 1975
The Vanishing Lichens

Rotberg R. I. 1971
Joseph Thomson and the exploration of Africa

Salt G. 1953
A Contribution to the Ecology of Kilimanjaro
J.Ecol. 42:375, 423-

Sinclair P. J. 1942-3
Kilimanjaro active
letters to the Times 24 Dec 1942; 5 May 1943

Smyth W. H. 1850
Presidential Address
Proc.Roy.Geog.Soc 20: 1x

Spink P. C. 1943
Volcanic activity on Kilimanjaro
Letters to the Times 24 April 1943; 18 Aug 1943

—1943
Glaciers in the Kilimanjaro crater
Quart.J.Roy.Met.Soc.

Swan L. W. 1961
The ecology of the high Himalayas
Sci.Am. 205(4):68-78

Tanzanian Notes and Records 1965
Vol 64: Commemorative Issue on Kilimanjaro

Tilman H. W. 1937
Snow on the Equator

Thomson J. 1880
Notes on the Geology of East Central Africa
Nature 1880:102

—1887
Through Masailand

Thornton R. 1864
Journey to Kilimanjaro
Proc.Roy.Geog.Soc. 9:15-16

—1865
Notes on a Journey to Kilimanjaro with von der Decken
J.Roy.Geog.Soc. 35:15

Vortisch H. 1954
Bahnbrecher in Afrika — Das Leben von J. L. Krapf

Wanless F. R. 1975
Spiders of the family Salticidae from the upper slopes of Everest and Makalu
Bull.Brit.Arach.Soc 3(5):132-136

Webb G. 1962
Top Dog (wild Dogs on Kilimanjaro)
Africana 2:21

Webster G. L. 1961
The altitudinal limits of vascular plants
Ecology 42:587-590

Whittow J. B. and Osmaston H. A. 1966
The deglaciations of the East African mountains
Occasional paper 3 of the Brit. Geomorphological Research Group.

Wilcockson K. 1967
Volcanoes

Index